The author

Jason Roscoe is a BABCP Therapist who runs his own private practice in Blackpool and is Lecturer in Cognitive Behavioural Therapy at the University of Cumbria.

Having previously worked in NHS Primary Care Mental Health Services for over seven years, Jason is highly experienced in assessing and treating people with anxiety difficulties. Trained in traditional cognitive-behavioural therapy, Jason has since developed specific interests in variants of CBT such as Acceptance and Commitment Therapy, Compassion-Focused Therapy and Schema Therapy which he incorporates into his work.

Jason now divides his time between medico-legal work, providing supervision to other therapists, seeing self-funding clients and lecturing.

Acknowledgements

I would like thank those that have inspired and supported me to feel able to write this book. Firstly, to dad – thank you for your unrelenting support, it is not unnoticed and is highly appreciated. To Fran – thank you for believing in me. To Evie, I hope you will be proud of me.

Finally I would like to thank Rufus for showing me the way and Mat for setting me on my way.

Contents

Introduction — 5

What is car travel anxiety? — 8

Part 1
Why have I not recovered already?

1. The logical brain versus the primitive brain — 12
2. The anxiety equation — 29
3. The need for total control and certainty — 33
4. Attentional bias — 35
5. The paradox of avoidance — 39
6. The problem with safety behaviours — 48

Part 2
What keeps my anxiety going?

7. Understanding the vicious cycle — 51
8. Unrelenting standards towards other road users — 58
9. The Toxic Trio of Anxiety maintenance — 62
10. Brain as a computer metaphor — 65

11. Barriers to change — 68

Part 3

The 1-2-3 way of managing anxious thoughts and feelings about driving and road travel

12. Thoughts are not facts – Theory A v Theory B — 72

13. Changing how we respond to our feelings — 83

14. Identifying your values and making changes — 90

Part 4

Maintaining your progress

15. Building on what you already learned — 101

16. Relapse Prevention — 106

17. Information for partners or family members — 110

18. Troubleshooting — 112

Glossary — 114

Appendices — 116

Introduction

The 1-2-3 approach

The 1-2-3 CBT guide to overcoming car travel anxiety has been written specifically for individuals who, following a road traffic accident have become 'stuck' in one way or another. What I mean by stuck is that perhaps you are scared of being in another accident and it is always on your mind or you may have become unable to relax in a car, constantly on the lookout for hazards and signs of bad driving. Maybe you are always telling your partner how they should drive and this is leading to arguments or that you feel that you are missing out not being able to go to certain places because of your anxiety about car travel.

This may cause you to feel as though you are driving yourself or those closest to you mad. What I can tell you is that far from being signs of madness, these thoughts and feelings and desire to escape or avoid are all completely normal and common human responses.

Whichever way travel anxiety affects you, Cognitive Behavioural Therapy (CBT) has been shown to help with many different anxiety problems and my 1-2-3 approach can help you reclaim your life by enabling you to:

1 – Learn about what is going on inside your brain and understand why you are struggling to overcome your anxiety

2- Learn ways to deal with your fears about road travel and of being in another accident

3- Help you identify what is important to you and how to start feeling and acting like *you* again

CBT is based on a simple premise - that our thoughts, feelings and behaviour are all interlinked and that making changes to how we respond to all three of them will improve our confidence as drivers or passengers.

Through the use of experiential exercises and case studies, my 1-2-3 approach will help you identify the thoughts that trouble you, the feelings you struggle with and the unhelpful things you do to cope with both of them. In addition to this I will get you to consider the consequences of always listening to what your mind tells you, to being on the run from your feelings and always behaving in the same old ways. Following that I will give you a range of options that you can use as you begin the journey towards becoming more confident as a driver and a passenger.

Having worked extensively with individuals who have been involved in road traffic accidents I have found that my take on CBT has helped many of them get back to feeling calm again behind the wheel or in the passenger's seat, something they never would have thought possible.

In this book I will be using techniques and ideas drawn from 'third wave' cognitive-behavioural therapies such as Acceptance and Commitment Therapy (ACT) and Compassion-focused Therapy (CFT) in addition to standard CBT.

Most self-help books will only show you how to understand and treat your travel anxiety from one CBT perspective. What I want to give you is the best of all of these evidence based approaches.

Finally, the 1-2-3 approach is a simple premise and because of this, most of my clients engage with it and start to feel significantly better after about six hourly sessions of therapy. By working through the same strategies you can expect to experience similar results by following the suggestions in the book. It is by no means an overnight fix however and will require lots of patience and commitment from you. Between appointments, my clients put into practice the new ways of thinking and behaving in cars as this is where the real changes take place.

Becoming 'mentally fit' requires the same level of attention as that of maintaining physical fitness where what we eat and how often we exercise is of paramount importance.
You might find that working through the book as pure self-help gets you to where you want to be or you may use the book to support and compliment a course of CBT that you are receiving.

If you are a therapist reading this book, you can use worksheets that I have placed in the appendices or you could recommend certain chapters for you clients to read as homework between sessions.

What is car travel anxiety?

The term 'car travel anxiety' is used to describe the thoughts, and feelings that are experienced by people who have begun to avoid or dread car journeys. This usually develops following a non-life threatening road traffic accident (RTA) where the person has either been a driver of a vehicle, a passenger or just witnessed an accident.

It is common to feel shaken up by an accident and to experience a loss of confidence behind the wheel for a few weeks afterwards however this book is written for those individuals who continue to feel anxious months, even years down the line.

Typical thoughts experienced by individuals with car travel anxiety are:

"I'll be in another crash if I drive on the motorway"

"The road is full of idiots these days"

"I can't relax, my heart is always racing when I'm in the car"

"What if the car in front of us suddenly slows down?"

Typical feelings are:

A churning stomach

Tight Chest

Racing heart

Typical ways of coping involve:

Giving the driver instructions / advice when you are a passenger in a car

Always being on the lookout for bad drivers

'Ghost' braking

Avoiding travelling or only driving on certain roads or at certain times of the day

Do these sound familiar? If so then it is likely that you are experiencing persistent car travel anxiety. You may have been told by your GP or a mental health professional if you have been assessed as part of an insurance claim that you are suffering from an adjustment disorder or a specific phobia of driving. A key feature of both of these is persistent travel anxiety and this book can help you overcome these difficulties.

Many of the features of car travel anxiety overlap with those of Post-traumatic Stress Disorder (PTSD) which is often more severe and requires treatment from a qualified and experienced CBT Therapist and therefore this book is not intended as a self-help method for PTSD.

The good news is that CBT is a very effective form of treatment for car travel anxiety. I shall explain how CBT works a bit later on in the book but what I would like to do first is help you understand why you have developed travel anxiety. Once you know what is keeping it going, you will then be in the position to decide if you are ready to change things.

I will be bringing the theory of 1-2-3 CBT to life by following the treatment journeys of two characters Dave and Susan who are both fictional but whose difficulties are representative of many of the clients that I have worked with and successfully helped reclaim their lives after car accidents.

Dave

Dave was involved in a four car collision on the motorway fourteen months ago. It happened as he indicated to come off at a junction and therefore neither he nor the other drivers involved were travelling at more than forty miles per hour. Dave's car was hit from the rear and he was then shunted into the car in front. Dave hurt his right knee in the accident and has had a course of physiotherapy to help regain movement and strength in the knee and surrounding muscles.

Dave had always believed that motorways were dangerous and he now avoids driving on them but will travel as a passenger, however he is always watching out for what other cars are doing and cannot relax. Dave notices that his heart beats very strongly when he is on the motorway and also gets sweaty palms. Dave is hooked on the fact that the accident shouldn't have happened and feels angry towards the driver he considers responsible for the accident. Dave spends a lot of time dwelling on 'if onlys'.

"If only I had taken the train in that day rather than driven"

"If only I had set off ten minutes earlier"

Dave feels compelled to give instructions and advice to his girlfriend Mel in order to prevent another accident from occurring but this behaviour usually leads to arguments as she feels undermined by him.

Susan

Susan was a front seat passenger in her husband's car when they were hit from the side by another vehicle who failed to give way at a junction. Although the impact was only at twenty miles per hour, Susan has gone from seeing driving as very safe to extremely dangerous and now spends a lot of time dwelling on the 'what if's and has done so in the eight months that have elapsed since the accident.

"What if he had been going faster?"

"What if I had of been seriously injured?"

Despite the accident occurring in a built up area within a town centre, Susan has become very anxious about travelling on motorways or roads where the speed limit is greater than thirty, so much so that she will avoid these where possible.

Whilst Dave and Susan's reactions may seem perfectly reasonable within the first few days or even weeks after the event, their *beliefs and behaviour* reflect a sense that they are still in danger and that another accident is highly likely.

Most people who have an accident that is non-life threatening will feel shook up for a number of weeks afterwards but will then gradually return to pre-accident functioning including driving or being a passenger on the same roads where their accident occurred.

What this book will show you is why Dave and Susan have got stuck on this 'chapter' of their lives. Hopefully you will be able to draw parallels between your own and their experiences and following their journey through therapy you will be able to use the same techniques to get you back to where you want to be.

Part 1

Why have I not recovered already?

1. The logical brain versus the primitive brain

I firmly believe that the first step to solving a problem is to understand what is keeping it going. To do this we need to have a basic appreciation of how our brain works in terms of our natural response to danger. This is step 1 of my 1-2-3 approach. Take a fire for example. We can spend lots of time trying to establish how it started but in the meantime its rages on and sets more things alight as it spreads. In order to stop it and eventually put it out we need to know what is *keeping it going* first and foremost. A fire needs a fuel source, it needs heat and it needs oxygen – take any one of these away and the fire will begin to wane and eventually go out. That might sound straight forward but the way our brain works is far from it yet we can compare a raging fire to strong, unwanted emotions like anxiety and anger. What I will show you in this book is both how they start following an RTA and how you can contain them enough to lead a fulfilling life.

An overview of the brain

Our brain is very complex and what I will be explaining in this book is a vast over-simplification of something we are still learning so much about.
 What you will learn in this book is enough about how our brain works to make sense of your own (and others) reactions to the world and how you can recognise and manage the natural conflict that we are faced with.

We start by using research from Compassion-focused Therapy (CFT) to look at the drives that our brain has which is to detect and eliminate threat (threat mode), to hunt and gather (our achievement mode) and to help us calm down and feel content (our soothing mode).

According to CFT theory, due to early life experiences some people have an overdeveloped threat mode and under-developed soothing mode which would usually counteract this. What this means in everyday life is that minor threats are perceived as massive threats to our existence and this person has very few ways of calming down the anxiety response that follows.

Dave had been brought up by parents that did not really discuss emotions and he learned from a very early age that he should 'man up' and not show any signs of upset. When Dave started to feel anxious about motorway journeys his brain ran the internalized 'programme' of him being 'a pussy' and he could hear his dad's voice telling him to 'grow a pair'. Dave criticized himself for feeling nervous about car journeys following his accident and he would feel incredibly guilty for avoiding motorways. When he did make himself travel on the motorway, he perceived his racing heart, rapid breathing and sweating to mean that he was not 'a man' and he would feel ashamed.

Dave found it really helpful to learn about the different modes of the brain and realized that the physical sensations he was experiencing were out of his control and not a sign of him being unmanly. He started to respond to himself with compassion by recognizing that his body's reaction was not something to feel ashamed about.

The job of the primitive brain

When it comes to making sense of our life experiences and regulating our emotional responses to them, there are three areas of the brain that are involved in this:-

- ❖ *the primitive brain* which we can might also refer to as the 'caveman brain'

- ❖ *the filing cabinet / processing centre.*

- ❖ *the logical brain* which we will say is the real you

In technical terms I am talking about the amygdala, the hippocampus and the pre-frontal cortex. I will now briefly describe the job that each of them has in sorting through our experiences and how they interact.

Amygdala (the caveman brain)

The amygdala is our brain's fear centre and is involved in triggering something called 'the fight or flight response'. This is essentially our alarm system that goes off whenever we are in real or imagined danger.

This is a mechanism that helped our ancestors survive because in caveman times we needed to be able to quickly decide if something was safe or dangerous and there were lots of things that could eat or poison us! Because of this, the ability to make snap decisions was key to our survival. Being able to generalize was also important and our ancestors may have concluded that " those purples berries are poisonous therefore anything purple that grows on trees could also be a danger to me".

The caveman brain is associated with quite a child-like view of the world. Situations are either safe or dangerous with no in-between.
It is characterized by hunches and gut feelings without a careful examination of facts. At times, this will save your life but you need to learn how to determine whether or not it is worth listening to.

Despite living in relatively safer times in the present day, our alarm can still be easily triggered by threats to our survival. Regardless of whether a threat is real or imagined, the body responds in the same way, setting off the fight or flight response as shown in Table 1.

Table 1

Examples of real threats	Examples of imagined threats
A car is about to imminently hit your car	What if that car didn't slow down and hit us?
Someone is about to attack you	You see someone who you think looks 'dodgy' but they walk past you innocently

There will be lots of false alarms when you are travelling in a car because your caveman brain will be imaging lots of bad things happening and it will be making mountains out of molehills when you see near misses or signs of bad driving. This will mean that your alarm will be going off frequently and you will be feeling as anxious as you would if something really happened.

Below is a list of physical sensations that occur when the fight or flight response is triggered. See how many you recognize from when you were last in a car or any other situations that you have found to be threatening.

- Increased heart rate
- Rapid breathing
- Sweaty palms
- Feeling hot
- Pins and needles in fingers and toes
- Tension in shoulders
- Shaking legs
- Racing thoughts
- The urge to escape from where you are

Although you might find some or all of these sensations unpleasant, they are all normal reactions that help prepare us to run away from danger or stay and fight it. Furthermore, anything in our environment that is a potential threat to us is shown to our amygdala first so that it can check out how serious the threat is before triggering this alarm. The amygdala does this by checking what is stored in the filing cabinet (the hippocampus). Like with the purples berries, if it is a 'match' then the alarm is triggered, sending lots of messages to different parts of our body to prepare us to run, fight or stay still until danger has passed.

The important thing to note here is that it does not have to be a direct match to set the alarm off. In order to ensure our survival, we have a very sensitive alarm that goes off whenever anything similar comes along which may be a danger to us, illustrated in Figure 1.

Figure 1 The sensitive alarm

TRIGGER

Yellow car

AMYGDALA CHECKS HIPPOCAMPUS FOR YELLOW CARS

Accident involved yellow motorbike

REACTION

Fight or flight response is set in motion resulting in a pounding heart, feeling hot and slightly out of breath. The urge to escape from the 'threat' emerges.

Hippocampus (the filing cabinet)

As you can see from Figure 1, the amygdala puts things into the hippocampus which it thinks we need to remember in order to stay alive. Anything yellow could set off an anxiety response in a person who was involved in an accident where the threat was a yellow motorbike. The hippocampus stores these as memories and our memories contain a mixture of information that has been created and elaborated by both the amygdala and the more rational part of our brain, the pre-frontal cortex.

The hippocampus helps us to make sense of our experiences and contextualize them, that is, put them into the order they occurred in our life and also to determine the importance of the experience. Many people are able to see a car accident (or other setbacks in life) as a one off bad experience that is unlikely to happen again.

As long as we believe that the accident is this massively important chapter in our life, the hippocampus will retain the memory as one that is highly significant and defines us. If we only have this way of thinking about the accident and of car travel situations stored in our filing cabinet then we will remain highly anxious.

Pre-frontal Cortex (the real you)

The pre-frontal cortex (here forth referred to as the cortex) is the part of our brain that we use to take a step back from situations and to look at things from different perspectives. In contrast to the amygdala which sees the world in black and white terms, the cortex deals in shades of grey. In evolutionary terms, it is fairly new kit . It is from the cortex where we can take an adult view of the world and the risks it poses to us. The cortex also contains the things that are important to us such as our interests and our values, something I shall be talking about in a lot more detail later on in the book.

The cortex may drive us to take risks because the things that are important to us cannot be achieved through staying nice and safe all of the time. Herein lies the inevitable conflict between the cortex and the amygdala – they want different things.

The amygdala does not care about our happiness, it just wants to keep us alive – at all costs. The cortex is concerned with our values and happiness and therefore realizes that this cannot happen without embracing the uncertainty that the pursuit of these values could end in tears. This contrast is shown in Figure 2 below.

Figure 2 – The dilemma

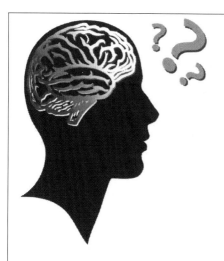 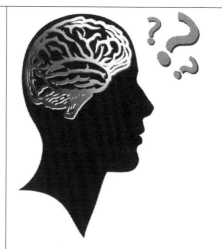

Caveman brain (amygdala) priorities

- Avoid danger
- Detect danger
- Escape from danger

Human brain (cortex) priorities

- Doing things that are fun
- Doing things that are meaningful
- Achieving goals

The problem is that people can start to legitimize their primitive brain's fears and believe that it is 'their' thoughts about the world which they are experiencing. Keeping themselves safe becomes their one and only value. What has happened is that the primitive brain has hijacked the controls and is now running the show. You have forgotten what you want from life and are only thinking about what you *do not want*.

The dilemma

Thoughts that come from the primitive brain are related to the detection and elimination of danger whereas thoughts that come from the new brain are linked to what is important to us, that is, our values. Sometimes they agree but most of the time they are at odds with each other. This is extremely important and will be the basis for starting to make changes to your life. When you wake in the morning you accept the risks that come from getting out of bed. You need to walk down the stairs to get breakfast to take away your hunger and to satisfy your taste buds. You are embracing the possibility of tripping up as you walk downstairs but you do so because it is important to you, not because it is risk free.

This is also your dilemma when it comes to recovering from car travel anxiety. Your primitive brain is shouting very loudly that you need to stay alive and eliminate all risks at all costs however in doing so you feel constantly anxious and you start to forget who you are and what you stand for.
This is a dilemma we all face if we want to live a fulfilling life. I will now show you how you can begin to manage this dilemma.

The role of our thoughts and emotions
Many of the thoughts that we have which come from the

primitive brain carry with them an evolutionary purpose. The need to survive long enough to pass on our genes leads us to be naturally risk averse and to 'play it safe' where possible. When we have an anxious thought for example, it is simply the primitive brain doing it's job – switching into threat mode and alerting us to possible danger. You may recognize this from when you think another car is too close to you and is going to hit you. As survival is our number one priority you instinctively blurt out to the driver, usually your nearest and dearest, some kind of expletives demanding that they stop or that they should have slowed down sooner.

To make sure we have paid attention to these potential threats to our survival, our brain also needs to send a very strong physical signal to us to make sure we act on the perceived risks; hence emotions such as fear are very powerful and difficult to ignore. The churning of the stomach, the racing heart, the sense of despair is often all-consuming and therefore we instinctively look inwards to see what they are telling us. This can make us susceptible to what is known as *emotional reasoning* which can be translated as 'I feel something bad is happening therefore it will happen'.

To make absolutely sure that these signals aren't easily dismissed, the brain facilitates time for reflection and for anticipating future risks and this is where worry and rumination come in.

The survival value of worry and rumination

Being able to think about our mistakes and near death experiences enables us to plan for how we can avoid them in the future, hence what is known as 'rumination', serves a useful purpose from a survival point of view.

Similarly, if we are able to anticipate future events that may threaten our survival (weather changes, animals that may prey on us, enemies that might attack us) then we have a better chance of sticking around long enough to pass on our genes. Worry allows us to consider what might happen and how we might deal with this.

Worry and rumination can be helpful in terms of our survival but beyond this they tend to make us fairly miserable if we get caught up in dedicating too much time to these primitive brain mental processes.

For Dave, he ruminated because he believed he should have set off earlier or that he should have got the train to work on the day of the accident. It is possible that Dave can learn from this rumination and that taking the train more often to work could ensure his survival. Unfortunately the cost of rumination to Dave is that he is often withdrawn from the people around him and he spends less time engaging in activities that would ordinarily make him feel good.

For Susan, worry felt like she was anticipating all of the different threats to her survival in the future and by doing so she could plan how to stay alive by avoiding driving at busy times and sticking to 'safe' quiet times. The downside of this is that Susan is constantly on edge, never able to relax and now avoids many activities that used to make her feel good.

The main take home message here is that worry and rumination are simply mental processes just as day dreaming, reminiscing and problem solving are. Learning to recognize when we are caught up in one of them gives us the opportunity to question how helpful they really are.

The fundamental problem is that people who become stuck with car travel anxiety either listen too much to the mental processes of worry and rumination or dedicate their lives to trying to escape from their anxious thoughts and feelings. In ACT the respective terms of these are 'fusion' and 'experiential avoidance'.

We don't have to listen to every thought we have

Most of the time we are living on auto-pilot, listening to repetitive thoughts without question and are responding to our emotions in predictable ways. This might not be a problem if the thoughts we were listening to and are accepting as gospel truth were life enhancing. If you are reading this book it is because your thoughts or the relationship you have with your thoughts are making your life a misery.

Imagine that you had the thought that the car you were in was made out of jelly. My guess is that you would either dismiss this thought straight away or momentarily consider it to be strange but then move your attention on to whatever it is you are doing.

Thoughts that we consider to be important take up our attention and this is called *fusion*. We *fuse* with thoughts that we think are important and we *defuse* from thoughts that we don't give much attention to. It is because you believe that your anxious thoughts are important that you fuse with them and in doing so you remain in threat mode. I have illustrated this as a process in Figure 3.

Figure 3

<u>Trigger</u>
My mind is telling me to scan the roads for danger

↓

<u>Fusion</u>
These thoughts keep me safe therefore I need to listen to them

↓

<u>Attention</u>
Become threat-focused

↓

<u>How I feel</u>
Anxious, Panicky, irritable

I call this 'snacking on mental junk food' and I will elaborate on this idea later in the book. What I want you to start noticing is your *emotional reasoning* and from this to consider that just because you think something it does not make it valid or important.

Just because you think you prevent further accidents by offering the driver advice does not mean that you are in reality making any difference whatsoever

Just because you think something bad is going to happen (such as another crash) does not mean it is.

Just because you think the world is full of bad drivers does not mean that this is the case

Becoming aware of how our thinking influences us

The primitive brain does not have time to think about the world in shades of grey therefore black and white thinking is the order of the day. On occasions this will save our lives but for most of the time it leads to biased interpretations such as the ones listed in Table 2.

Table 2

Thinking error	Examples
❖ Black and white thinking (also referred to as 'all or nothing' thinking	I am either TOTALLY safe in the car OR I am in grave danger
❖ Jumping to conclusions	That car WOULD have hit us if I hadn't of told you to slow down
❖ Catastrophising	Any trip on the motorway will lead to a CRASH
❖ Magnification and minimization	The road is FULL of bad drivers
❖ Personalisation	I'm an unlucky person, if anyone will be in another crash its bound to be ME
❖ Emotional reasoning	I FEEL like we're going to be in an accident therefore we should avoid driving today

Which ones do you identify with?

_____

There are more of these errors in thinking cited in CBT literature but these are the main ones at play when you are in threat mode and the ones which I want you to start to spot when you think about car travel or when you are travelling by car.

Although your day to day thoughts will change depending on the situation you are in, all of your anxious thoughts about car travel can be put under one of more of these errors in thinking. As you get better at spotting them, you will begin to see how repetitive they are and can be seen as *stories* that your mind produces every time you encounter what it believes to be a threat.

Taking a step back from our thoughts

In Cognitive Therapy (CT), the content of our thoughts was seen to be the problem such as the content of what we are worrying or ruminating over. Anxious individuals experience dysfunctional thoughts which are distortions of reality and modification of these thoughts allows the individual to see the world more clearly and thus their distress dissipates.

In Acceptance and Commitment Therapy (ACT), the content of thoughts is irrelevant; it is how much attention the individual gives to these thoughts (and mental processes) that counts. When a person fuses with a particular thought, they have become hooked on it and this pulls them away from doing things that would improve their lives and help them learn that they are not in as much danger as they believe themselves to be.

ACT incorporate mindfulness practices to help individuals unhook themselves from their thoughts. Mindfulness might be a term that you have heard or you may not be familiar with this at all. Put simply, mindfulness involves being aware of what is going on in the here and now, moment to moment and this is incredibly helpful for people when it comes to taking a step back from what they are thinking and doing day in, day out.

Whilst I am generally an advocate of mindful approaches, the only concern I have about rigidly sticking to one school of thought here is that if we still continue to believe that our thoughts are true for example 'I'm going to die', 'I'm an unlucky person' then we will find it very difficult to just use mindfulness with them. In light of this, I believe that using Cognitive Therapy (CT) with some clients initially is helpful to weaken their beliefs in the validity of their thoughts before moving on to using mindfulness strategies.

I have used both ACT and CT approaches with many travel anxious clients to good effect however I do not see one as being more credible or superior than the other. What they both have in common is that they are teaching people to develop *meta-cognitive awareness* (that is, to think about their thoughts rather than blindly accept them). They are also teaching people that they do not have to become slaves to their thoughts and their feelings.

The 1-2-3 way of handling anxious thoughts

One of the most important steps in developing meta-cognitive awareness is beginning to spot negative thoughts such as those experienced by Dave and Susan.

It is then about developing the skill of taking a step back from them, what is referred to in ACT as defusion and more generally as *'de-centering'*. I will show you how to do this and also how to play detective, noticing the thoughts that make you feel anxious and fearful by labelling what is wrong with them.

The second stage is to challenge them and to become good at 'putting them on trial'. The third stage is when we can start to spot these thoughts a mile off, noticing that they are variants of the same stories that our mind plays on a loop. By learning to 'name the story', we can start to label them and because we know them and have challenged them a hundred times before we can just begin to notice (defuse from them) and let them be (using mindfulness skills). You will then be in a position to do the things that you want with your life without being held back by your worries.

Summary

Now that you know about the conflict in all human brains between wanting safety and pursuing things of value to us you will be wondering why you are caught up in this struggle more so than perhaps other people that you know. You will no doubt have friends, family members, work colleagues who have experienced road traffic accidents so why don't they worry about being in another accident as much as you do?

The next few chapters will help shed some light on why you have become stuck with travel anxiety and give you some ideas about how to move forward with your life.

2 The anxiety equation

Anxiety has been described as an equation, consisting of four separate but interacting variables and which I shall illustrate in Figure 4 with several examples. If we remove any one of them then this can reduce or remove the *heightened* anxiety that we feel in response to any given situation.

Figure 4

How likely I think it is that it will happen x How bad I predict it will be
Whether I think I can cope with it or not + Who or what can help me in this situation

Dave thinks that if he travels on the motorway then there is a high possibility that he will be in a crash. He believes this will be fatal or near fatal and that his life would be completely ruined if he didn't die there and then.

Dave's anxiety equation looked like this:

If I drive on the motorway I will definitely be in a crash x It will be fatal or I'll be in a wheelchair from the injuries
I would go to pieces and be miserable for the rest of my life + my girlfriend would leave me and I'd be without a job or anything to fill my time

We can call this 'Theory A' and I shall explain this in more detail later in the book. Based on these predictions, it is no wonder the idea of driving on the motorway fills Dave with dread to the point that he always avoids doing it.

Susan on the other hand does not believe there is much likelihood of her having another car crash however she thinks that if it did happen it would be awful. She would not be able to cope and because of this it feels easier and safer to just travel by bus now.

Susan's anxiety equation looked like this:

$$\frac{\textit{Not very likely I'll be in another accident} \times \textit{The hassle would be too much – I would lose my mind}}{\textit{I would not cope with all the hassle of insurance claims} + \textit{I would be left on my own to deal with everything that comes from it}}$$

Different parts of the anxiety equation will be stronger for some people than others and we need to offer different interventions accordingly.

Dave worked out with his therapist that he had been a passenger in a car or a driver approximately 15,000 times in his life and had only been in one accident. They then discussed how 1 in 3 people are diagnosed with cancer yet he did not spend much time at all dwelling on the possibility of getting cancer. Reappraising the likelihood of being in another crash played a part in reducing Dave's anxiety about future car travel more than it did for Susan. Whenever he thought about being in another accident he reminded himself of the likelihood of it occurring – this became 'Theory B'.

In clinical practice I have worked with clients who feel much better when they consider the likelihood of being in another crash whereas for others the worst part is living with the uncertainty that it could happen no matter how unlikely. For this reason, different strategies are required.

Susan and her therapist worked on her perception of how she would cope in the unlikely event of another accident occurring. By discussing her options through problem solving, Susan was able to see that she might find it a hassle but she has the knowledge and emotional support around her to be able to manage.

I would like you to have a go at writing out what you think your anxiety equation would look like by considering the following questions.

How likely do I think it is that I'll be in another accident?

If I was in another accident, what is the most likely outcome of it?

How do I think I would cope with it at the time and afterwards?

Who or what could help me deal with the situation?

Figure 5

My anxiety equation

$$\frac{x}{+}$$

3. The need for total control and certainty

Difficulty tolerating uncertainty has been shown to be a factor in many anxiety problems and car travel anxiety is a classic example of this.

For many clients like Susan, they realize that the chance of being in another car crash is a slim one yet they do not want to take the risk that it might happen. For them, the possibility is too awful as they often believe the next one will be much worse or that they would not be able to cope with the hassle of the insurance claim again.

These individuals are sacrificing living a full life because they cannot accept the uncertainty of being in another accident. This need for certainty leads them to assume too much responsibility as a passenger and often without intending to, they undermine the abilities of the driver by insisting that they need to keep a look out for dangers on the road and offer lots of advice or criticism as a means of keeping themselves safe.

The need to feel certain, rather than actually being certain (which is impossible), leads people to needing to be in control of their environment. They will often state that they feel out of control if they are travelling as a passenger or they will struggle with not being in control of the decisions made by drivers of other cars on the road.

Relinquishing control

Relinquishing this control is about putting your trust back in others and in the context of car travel, it is about trusting the driver and other car drivers judgments.

The accident that you experienced may have shaken up what you believe about car travel. Like Susan, you may have previously thought of it as a fairly safe form of transport and this assumption has now been called into question. This had led to a complete shift from "I'm completely safe" to "I'm always in danger". Similarly, the accident may have confirmed a prior belief like that of Dave's, that the roads are dangerous and you daren't take another chance.

Both of these represent a very child-like view of the world and are characteristic of the primitive brain's black and white thinking. As an adult you know that we cannot be certain about most things in life and that the roads cannot but full of bad drivers due to the relatively low numbers of crashes that happen in relation to car journeys.

It is very likely that you put your trust in others on a daily basis in non-car related situations. You trust that the people who have prepared your food in a café or restaurant have taken certain steps to ensure that your meal is safe to eat. You might even trust bus drivers, train drivers, taxi drivers. The point is, that nothing in life is certain and you know this at some level and you tolerate uncertainty more than you are aware.

Only by starting to trust car drivers again will your primitive brain learn that you are not still in danger. This might involve you letting your partner drive if you are insisting on doing all of the driving or it might involve you travelling as a passenger with several of your friends and family members so that you can begin to trust drivers again.

4. Attentional bias

Imagine a tea strainer where only the coloured water is let through and the tea leaves remain on the other side of the strainer. A similar thing is happening with your driving experiences. Only certain bits of your driving experience are getting through which are those that 'match' how you view yourself and other road users and those that don't are kept out. Over time you can imagine what effect this has.

The capacity to filter out information in this way is related to our strong need for survival. We pay attention to danger and exclude signs of safety. This will save our life if we are clearly in danger but it does not work so well when it relates to car travel. Car travel has some inherent dangers – yet most of the time you reach your destination safely. For individuals with car travel anxiety, you are only noticing signs of danger and are excluding all of the information which tells you that you are fairly safe. This process is called 'schemas bias' and is illustrated below.

Figure 6 - Dave's schema bias

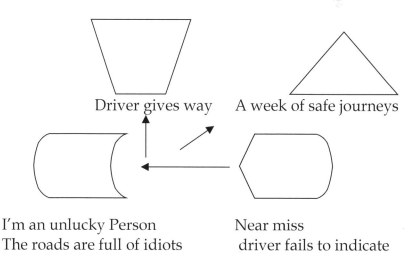

As you can see from the illustration, looking at the world through these lenses, positive driving experiences such as those represented by the triangle and trapezoid are discounted, trivialised or forgotten about (and usually do not occur often enough due to avoidance) whilst neutral things go largely unnoticed. Negative experiences that fit into the belief system are taken as proof that the roads are a highly dangerous place, only bad things happen to them and the future is bleak.

Does this sound familiar? If so, I would like you to try to draw out your own schema bias so that you can see the information that you take as proof of your ongoing danger and the information that you miss which tells you that you are relatively safe.

Clients often say to me that you only have to watch the news or read the newspapers to see what a dangerous place the world is, however, by keeping a running tally of negative experiences this serves to reinforce the above beliefs. 'There's another example of my luck / how bad the world is / how nothing will change', "Not again!" "What next?!"

This line of thinking is not unreasonable if you are convinced the world is a dangerous place, that you are in danger and that nothing will ever change. It is however a distorted view where only events, experiences or information that fits their beliefs are filtered into the person's awareness. Is it any wonder that you then feel bad when you keep telling yourself these things?

The self-perpetuating nature of travel anxiety

The longer a person avoids certain roads or travel conditions, the stronger their belief becomes that the way they view themselves, the world and the future is correct and factual.

Susan for example had avoided roads with speed limits greater than 30mph since her accident. This meant that she had no experiences to challenge her schema bias and therefore her belief that those roads are dangerous was maintained over many months.

What I would like you to begin to do is observe your car travel from a more objective standpoint. This forms part of step 2 of my 1-2-3 approach. Now that you are aware of your own schema bias in action, I want you to set up a competing way of filtering information. I want you to begin to gather evidence of safety and of good driving.

Looking for the rose in a field of nettles (mindfulness)

This is something I tell all my clients to do, especially those suffering with persistent low mood and chronic depression but it can also be effectively applied to travel anxiety. I would like you to look for the rose in the field of nettles at least once on every car journey. This is not about telling you to think positive and all will be well, it is about training your mind to look at the world in a more objective way. Rather than thinking a glass is half full rather than half empty, we are aiming to look at a glass having 250ml of water in a 500ml glass. To develop this skill we can manipulate where we zoom our camera on to and in relation to travel anxiety, your camera is always zoomed in on signs of danger. Whilst spotting the rose will not take away the reality of dangers on the road, it may help you to realise that the roads are not 100%, 24/7 danger-filled places.

Here are some ideas for the roses to look out for…..

Signs of safe driving in others

Signs of courteous driving in others

If you wish to try this more generally in your life then look out for....

Your child's laugh or smile
The smell of a favourite scent
The warmth of a shower
The taste of a favourite food

The positive experiences of driving log is a way of recording experiences which challenge your schema bias and allow you to view car travel from a more balanced perspective. Susan decided to complete this so that she could show herself all of the times where she travels without being in danger.

Worksheet 1 - Excerpt from Susan's Positive Experiences of Driving Log

Day and time	Driving situation	Observations
Wednesday 2.00pm	Travelling as a passenger along a previously avoided A road with a 50 mph speed limit	Everyone appeared to be sticking to the speed limit

5. The paradox of avoidance

The function of avoidance

It is in our nature to avoid things which are unpleasant or harmful to us, whether that is plants which are poisonous, extremes of heat or cold, hunger and physical injury. Regardless of whether the threat is real or imagined, avoidance is a very simple and sometimes effective solution.

Take people with flying phobia or snake phobia for example. All you have to do is avoid zoos or countries where you are likely to encounter snakes or avoid getting on a plane or helicopter and the problem is solved. This might inconvenience you, having to go on holiday by boat or restricting your holidays to destinations where can take the train but you can learn to live it. In a similar way, most of us in the western world don't come into contact with snakes much in our day to day existence therefore again, it is easy to avoid the thing that makes you feel afraid.

That said, it is difficult to avoid any associations with flying or snakes because we will always have friends or family members enthusiastically telling us about their holidays and their experiences flying or being in airports. Television programmes or films may feature scenes where the characters are on a plane or we might catch a glimpse of a wildlife documentary that shows snakes in their natural habitat or a presenter holding a snake. This is where the holes in the avoidance solution begin to appear.

It is almost completely impossible to avoid road travel as most of us get in cars to commute to work or to go to another part of the country to see our friends or relatives.

Other forms of avoidance

Sometimes the main reason for avoidance of certain situations is more to do with the way it makes a person feel rather than their belief that something bad will happen. Generally speaking, the less distress tolerant a person is, the more likely they are to avoid situations which trigger uncomfortable thoughts and feelings.

Dave found the physical sensations of anxiety that he experiences on motorways to be particularly unacceptable. He dreaded the racing heart and being sweaty made him want to avoid these situations as often as he could. If he had to endure a motorway journey, Dave would be pre-occupied with controlling his level of anxiety and would sometimes take beta-blockers or he would try to take slow deep breaths which a friend had told him would help.

Susan on the other hand was less bothered by her 'fight or flight' sensations and the fear of being in another crash was the worst part of car travel for her.

What is a paradox?

We keep using control methods and avoidance because they work – in the short term. Anti-depressants, alcohol, thought blocking, distraction all work for a few hours, days, weeks or even months but ultimately they fail because they do not get rid of the things we are trying to escape from.

Conversely, if we make room for the very feelings and thoughts that we don't want, something different happens. They lose their power over us.

Just as the tide goes out when it is ready to, just as a windy day passes in its own time, emotions such as sadness, anger, and fear will all pass without the need to make them go away if only we give them chance to rise and fall. This is called a paradox and what we can learn from this paradox is that we must try a different approach with our thoughts, emotions and physical sensations to that which we use to escape from other threats.

Exercise 1

Try holding a piece of paper or a book at arm's length with your arms fully extended, pushing the object as far away from your body as possible. I want you to do this for a minute and whilst you are doing this, I want you to notice the tension in your arms, the effort involved in pushing it away and the amount of your attention this takes up. Does this feel similar to what you are doing with unwanted thoughts, emotions or physical sensations?

Now, lay the piece of paper on your lap. Notice that you have not gotten rid of the piece of paper yet the struggle has gone. Based on an ACT concept called 'unworkable action' I want you to list all of the things that you have tried since the accident to rid yourself of emotional 'bad weather' that is, times when you experience low motivation, worry, fear, anger, guilt, sadness, self-criticism. I have put forward some suggestions and ask you to consider how long it worked for when you tried it.

In Worksheet 2, I want you to consider how you deal with these unwanted thoughts and feelings at present as I will be offering an alternative way of dealing with them in Part Three of the book.

Worksheet 2

Things I have done to rid myself of accident related thoughts, emotions and physical sensations	How long it worked for _____ days / weeks / months
1. Antidepressant medication 2. Avoiding places or people that trigger certain thoughts 3. Tried to distract myself whilst in the car 4. Insisted on family members or friends always being around me or sitting in specific seats in the car	

Hopefully you can see the futility of the control agenda. Despite trying many different methods to make your unwanted thoughts and feelings about car travel go away you continue to be stuck with them or you are successful at making them go away through the use of drugs or alcohol but the cost of this to your life is too great.

Whatsmore, by responding to our *clean discomfort* with a struggle we inadvertently turn this into *dirty discomfort* as illustrated in Figure 7.

Figure 7

'CLEAN' DISCOMFORT WHEN TRAVELLING BY CAR
(racing heart / anxious thought / bad memory)

STRUGGLE WITH IT
(Question why it is happening / try to stop it / dull it down

CREATE 'DIRTY' DISCOMFORT
(physical feelings become stronger, thoughts stick around)

STRUGGLE EVEN MORE
(Up the attempts to control / block or remove thoughts and feelings through avoidance)

CREATE EVEN MORE 'DIRTY' DISCOMFORT
(physical feelings become even stronger, thoughts stick around longer)

By struggling even more to get rid of your (now) dirty discomfort, you will inevitably look for more ways to shut out these thoughts and feelings. In clients with travel anxiety this means avoiding more and more busy roads, spending more time at home and increasingly living a life that is far removed from how they would like it to be.

The struggle leads to a shrinking of the sphere in which they operate. If you imagine a large circle represents the things they used to do and places they used to go, the tiny circle represents the narrow sphere that they reduce their life to because of the drive to avoid unwanted thoughts, emotions and physical sensations.

Figure 8

Full and meaningful life   v Life governed by drive to avoid

I want you to consider how much your circle has shrunk because of your attempts to avoid feeling anxious in the car or to avoid the possibility of being in another accident.

Summary of the control agenda

1. We do not get to learn what would happen if we did put ourselves in that situation and we don't learn that we can cope with difficulties

2. We miss out on experiences that will enrich our lives as we try to avoid and block more and more

3. We intensify unwanted thoughts and feelings by struggling with them (turning clean discomfort into dirty discomfort.

In what ways are defusion and blocking different?

At first glance, defusion can seem like another form of blocking and this is a confusion that I regularly have to clear up with clients. Whilst defusion is ultimately about letting thoughts go it is not a desperate and hurried attempt to make them go away instantly in the way that distraction or thought blocking are. In defusion we are allowing thoughts to just be, recognizing them as transient mental events and then getting on with what is important to us. In distraction all we can think about is the thought or the feeling that we want rid of and we may push it out of our mind for a short time but then it comes bouncing back in with a vengeance.

The case for an acceptance-based approach to unwanted thoughts and feelings

In contrast to the control agenda, the acceptance agenda means accommodating our unwanted thoughts and feelings which may seem counter-intuitive - it goes against everything we would normally do when we are in pain and are suffering. Hopefully you will have seen that escape and avoidance are short lived and ultimately futile. This does not mean that you are doomed to be stuck in the depths of despair for the rest of your life though. The solution just takes a bit of getting used to.

Accepting and accommodating our unwanted thoughts, emotions and physical sensations is about learning to live with clean discomfort and giving up the fight about it. This can be beneficial in at least two ways. The first is that they lose their power over us when we stop struggling with them and allow them to 'lodge' with us. The second is that by getting to know them better we can perhaps learn more about them and what they are trying to tell us.

Often we have certain thoughts and emotions for good reason and therefore blocking them out all of the time means that we may miss out on vital information that our brain and body are trying to tell us.

Managing the conflicting needs of the brain

We have established that the primitive brain and the logical brain (you) have different needs and different priorities and that they usually clash rather than agree. In any conflict situation we need to negotiate and reach a compromise. In doing so the primitive brain or the logical brain must 'back down' and accept that there will be a trade off.

Competing needs – you can't have your cake and eat it

If you want to enjoy life, you need to learn to compromise and accept risk and uncertainty. It really does boil down to a decision between risk and rewards. The primitive brain and the logical brain rarely agree and have different priorities. The primitive brain shouts the loudest and prefers worry and rumination as it's way of navigating through life but this is not you and does not represent what you want.

Being aware of this puts you in a very powerful position and is the beginnings of developing skills in something called *meta-cognitive awareness*. Put simply, Meta-cognition is being able to take a step back from or adopt a helicopter view of your thoughts. Experienced practitioners of mindfulness are likely to have highly developed meta-cognitive awareness.

In Part Three I will be introducing you to the importance of values and clarifying values as this will be your pot of gold at the end of the rainbow. This is step three of my 1-2-3 approach and will involve moving towards rather than away from situations, thoughts and feelings that you have been avoiding in order to live a value-congruent life. The key message here is that you can't have your cake and eat it. It is impossible to feel totally safe and certain and live a rich and meaningful life.

6. The problem with safety behaviours

Safety behaviours are one of the main reasons why you have not yet overcome your car travel anxiety yet they are the very things that you believe keep you from having another accident. A safety behaviour is something that we do which we feel protects us in some way and they are incredibly addictive – we keep on doing them because they seem to prevent the bad thing from happening.

Here are some common safety behaviours that people with car travel anxiety use on a regular basis

- Holding tightly to the car seat
- Distraction
- Watching out for bad driving / hazards on the road
- Giving instructions / advice to the driver
- Only travelling at certain times of the day
- Insisting on doing all of the driving

Susan believed that the reason she had not been in another crash was because she was looking out for hazards whilst a passenger in her husband's car. When the therapist asked her who kept her husband safe when he drove on his own, she was flummoxed as she had not stopped to consider this before.

The inherent problem with safety behaviours is that they provide us with an *illusion of total safety*. Even if we give advice / instructions to the driver, even if we only travel on limited speed roads - we are not guaranteed to avoid accidents.

To recap a point I made earlier - Life is full of risks. Getting out of bed involves risk. Walking down the stairs involves risk.

Most of us travel on trains, ferries and airplanes not because they are risk free but because we want the holiday or the day trip at the end of it. What I want you to consider is all of the risks that you face in life which you tolerate because you know that total safety is impossible but also because what you are taking the risk for is worth it.

Situations I put myself in day to day where there are risks involved

_____

_____

How do I deal with this uncertainty that something bad might happen?

_____

_____

_____

_____

Justifying avoidance

Human beings will do almost anything to avoid discomfort and sometimes this involves telling ourselves things that we want to believe.
In the context of car travel anxiety, this can mean justifying our avoidance of certain driving situations with an excuse dressed up as a valid reason.

Dave would tell himself and others that he had always disliked driving on the motorways at weekends because it was too busy and this annoyed him more than it made him anxious.

Whilst this could be true, someone whose primary motive was to avoid a place because of annoyance would put themselves through it if it meant there was something important that they were trying to achieve. The person who is predominantly anxious will usually talk themselves and others out of doing the journey even if it is somewhere they would like to go.

What types of avoidance do I justify to myself?

_____

_____

_____

Section Summary

1. Understand the natural conflict that exists in our minds

2. Learn how to accept and manage the primitive mind

3. Commit to abandoning 'unworkable action'

Part 2

What keeps my anxiety going?

7. Understanding the vicious cycle

You are what you think

As I mentioned at the start of the book, in CBT, our over-arching theory is that *you are what you think* or you are what you *make of* what you think. Most people instinctively believe that it is the things that happen to them in life that affects how they feel emotionally. The car breaks down so they feel angry, their partner doesn't arrive home when they say they will so they feel worried, the job interview goes badly so they feel sad.

Whilst this is true to some extent, that these emotions would not have arisen had it not been for those events, it is far from being the whole story as I shall explain further.
To begin with I want to introduce you to the thinking-feeling-behaviour link so you can see how certain thoughts influence emotions and how our behaviour often reinforces unwanted thoughts and feelings.

We have already looked at these components separately and now I want to show you how they are linked together. The attentional bias that you have towards signs of bad driving lead you to believe that you are still in danger when travelling by car. Your safety behaviours that make you feel better in the short term, prevent you from learning that they are unnecessary and that another accident is unlikely.

Finally, your difficulties tolerating uncertainty mean that rather than taking the chance, you withdraw from journeys that you consider to be risky and your life starts to shrink. Let me give you an example of this using Dave's story.

Dave had been involved in a car crash on the motorway fourteen months ago. He has not driven on the motorways since and prefers to be a passenger even on local journeys. His partner Mel suggests that they drive on the motorway to go and see his relatives for the day.

Dave's *negative automatic thoughts* in response to this are:

"We'll be in a crash if we go on the motorway. Its best to stick to the A roads"

"Why is she suggesting that, she knows how I feel about the motorway?"

"What if I have a panic attack and freak out in the car?"

Because Dave accepts these thoughts to be facts, he feels initially angry then anxious (emotional response). His heart begins to pound in his chest and his jaw feels tight (physical response). He tells Mel that they need to go on the A roads even though it will take much longer. Reluctantly, Mel agrees to this to avoid an argument. Whilst they are driving, Dave is in the front passenger seat and engages in 'ghost braking' whenever he thinks Mel is driving too fast or they approach a junction. He also points out hazards to Mel such as other cars going too fast (safety behaviour).

The diagram overleaf illustrates how Dave's thoughts, feelings and behaviours are mutually reinforcing.

Figure 9 - Interaction between thoughts, emotions and behaviour

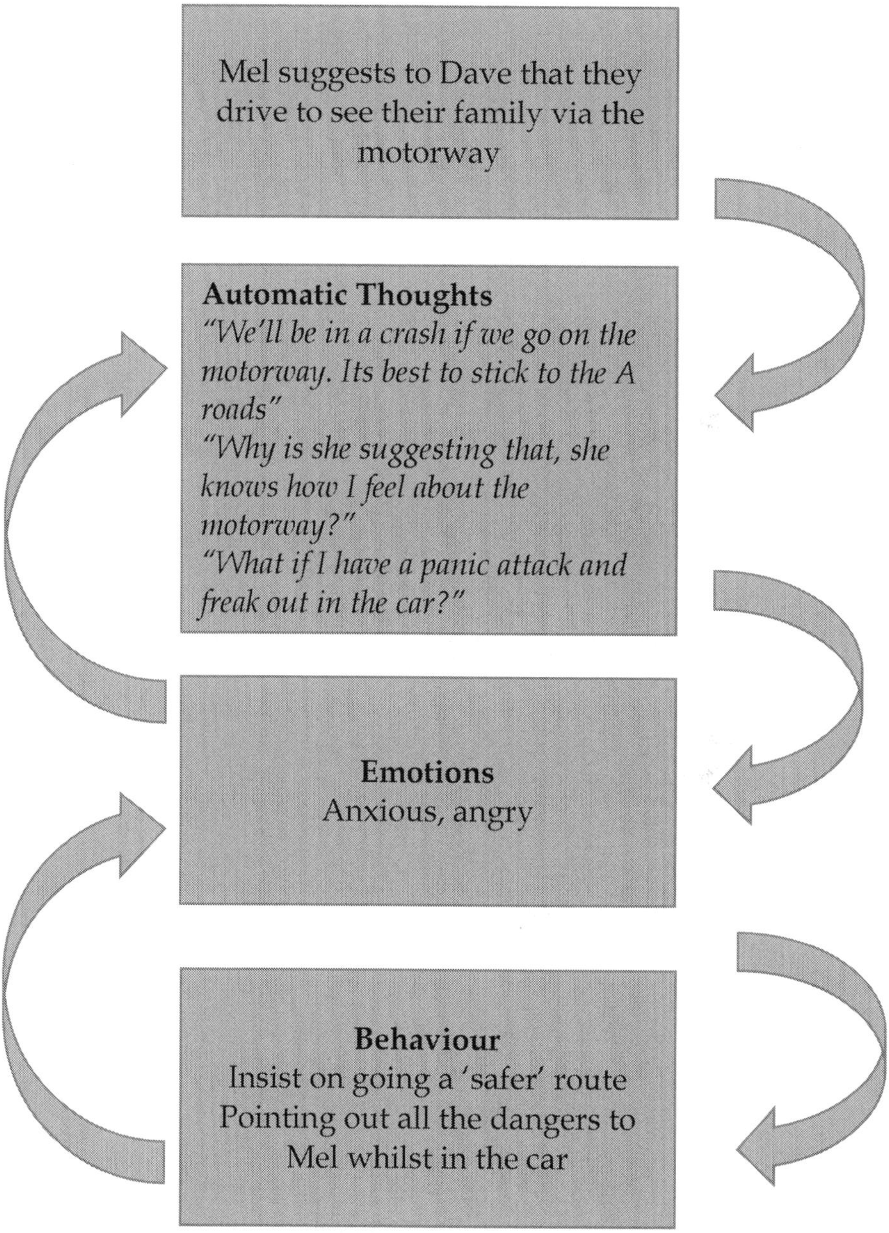

Mel suggests to Dave that they drive to see their family via the motorway

Automatic Thoughts
"We'll be in a crash if we go on the motorway. Its best to stick to the A roads"
"Why is she suggesting that, she knows how I feel about the motorway?"
"What if I have a panic attack and freak out in the car?"

Emotions
Anxious, angry

Behaviour
Insist on going a 'safer' route
Pointing out all the dangers to Mel whilst in the car

The arrows going down show how one leads to the other whereas the arrows pointing upwards show how certain parts are reinforced, for example, Dave's avoidance of his anxious feelings and of the motorway cause friction between him and Mel but more importantly, reinforce his emotions of anxiety and anger and prevent him from testing out the validity of his predictions.

Whilst Dave would not have had these thoughts or feelings if Mel had of not suggested driving on the motorway, it was not Mel who caused Dave to think these thoughts. Furthermore, whilst Dave felt better in the short term for avoiding the motorway and giving Mel instructions about the hazards he could see, this did not take away his anxiety.

How else might Dave have responded to the situation?

If Dave had tried to take a step back from his negative automatic thoughts he might have thought instead that:

"I have only been in one crash out of the 15,000 car journeys I've had in my life. This tells me that another one is highly unlikely"

This is called *cognitive restructuring* or thought challenging and is a standard component of CT treatment. This alternative thought helped Dave change his anxiety equation by reappraising the likelihood of another crash. Dave needed to do some further cognitive restructuring around other parts of the anxiety equation to help him feel less anxious about car journeys.

Alternatively Dave might have used an ACT approach to his thoughts such as *defusion* by considering how many times this thought (or variations of it) has popped into his head in all of the car journeys he has been in since the accident and labelled it as *the 'I'm a danger magnet" story* rather than getting hooked by it each and every time it resurfaces.

Past experiences

We can make sense of Dave's response to car journeys by looking at his childhood and travel history.

Dave had an anxious mother who was always telling him to be careful when he was driving and regularly told him about all the accidents she had heard about on the telly and radio. When Dave was a child he always remembered his mother worrying about something and this communicated the idea that the world was a dangerous place. This made him vulnerable to being on the lookout for being danger on the roads. Dave had also been involved in another, less serious accident in his early twenties, Whilst it is understandable from these defining experiences that Dave has these worries in his road journeys, his behaviour and ways of thinking are not inevitable.

Unintended consequences

There were several types of unintended consequences for Dave in his efforts to keep himself safe post-accident. His confidence in being on the motorway did not improve (cognitive consequence), his behaviour of continually finding fault in Mel's and other people's driving had put a strain on their relationship (interpersonal consequence) and he felt sad, angry and anxious much of the time (emotional consequences).

Reflecting on the various consequences of your behaviour is something I will be asking you to look at repeatedly throughout this book. What I would like you to do now is have a go at drawing out your own formulation based on a recent example of when you have been in the car or someone suggested a car journey and you reacted with dread or avoidance.

Worksheet 3 - My formulation of how my thoughts, emotions and behaviour are linked

What this example highlights is how our thoughts if left unchecked can negatively influence how we feel and behave, not the event itself. Although Dave would not have felt angry and anxious had Mel reacted in the way he wanted her to, it was his interpretation of the situation and his reaction to his interpretation that produced his unwanted emotions. It also shows that an ACT or CT approach consisting of either labelling (defusing) or examining and modifying thoughts can change the end result (how he feel and how his relationship progresses).

My view and this appears to be supported by research comparing different cognitive and behavioural methods, is that it is not important how we detach from our thoughts, the main thing is that we find a way that works for us, hence me advocating a range of CBT approaches that you can use.

8. Unrelenting standards towards other road users

A world without any standards would be chaos not doubt and most people will agree that there needs to be some consensus around what constitutes good enough and safe driving.

Some people however have extremely high and inflexible standards that they impose upon themselves and others which are difficult to live up to all of the time. This is a form of perfectionism where there is no margin for human error that is accommodated for in these standards and this becomes a source of rumination for these people.

Dave held inflexible rules around how others road users 'should' and 'should not' drive. This meant that when they were obeying his rules he felt calm and happy but when people inevitably breached them, he reacted his anger and frustration.

The perspective shift

Many people like Dave with unrelenting standards become consumed by irritation, bitterness and anger because they cling to *'absolutes'* which according to Rational Emotive Behaviour Therapy is a rigid belief system about how the world *should* be. This is again, a rather child-like fantasy view of life and once we look at the world from our adult perspective and can truly accept that nothing 'should' be the case, we can then free ourselves up to experience life for all its ups and downs.

When we truly learn to accept how the world is, how we are, how others are - we can then stop trying to control the tide and instead commit our energies to the things that we *can* change.

If you do recognize perfectionism in yourself towards other road users then I would suggest that you consider the pros and cons of holding these beliefs the high and perhaps unreasonable expectations that you impose like Dave has done in the example below.

I would then ask you to consider the consequences for you of holding on to these standards

Worksheet 4 – Dave's cost-benefit analysis of perfectionism

Advantages of perfectionist standards towards other road users	Disadvantages of perfectionist standards towards other road users
I feel like I can set a standard for others to follow and I can point out to people the times when they are driving dangerously	*Leads to arguments with family, friends and occasionally road rage* *It means I feel wound up a lot of the time and can't enjoy car journeys*

Dave decided that although he preferred it if people drove in ways that he thought were the right way, holding this view rigidly caused him too many problems in terms of getting angry with strangers and with Mel.

Dave came up with a more flexible rule by considering that because the number of crashes on roads were low in comparison to the number of car journeys made then it might be that other drivers knew how to drive safely for the most part even if they did not share the same views as him.

Worksheet 4 – My Cost-benefit analysis of perfectionism

Advantages of perfectionist standards towards other road users	Disadvantages of perfectionist standards towards other road users

What is the interpersonal consequence of continuing to think in this way? (what effect does it have on my relationships?)
What is the emotional consequence of continuing to think in this way? (what feelings keep showing up?)

What is the cognitive consequence of continuing to fuse with this story? (how does this affect my world view / the way I think about others and the future?)

If you have decided to change I want you to write down a more flexible perspective to hold about the world and other people.

My new rules about other people's driving to live by

_____

_____

_____

_____

9. The Toxic Trio of Anxiety maintenance

You can think of your car travel anxiety as having three components – what you say to yourself and do before, during and after car journeys. I call this the toxic trio and this is what we shall be looking at changing, to help you learn to enjoy or at least tolerate car journeys again.

People with car travel anxiety use lots of safety behaviours and tend to worry in advance of car journeys. They will often picture in their minds eye, a terrible version of events that will unfold, sometimes imagining a crash taking place. They will tend to plan (safety behaviour) how they will avert danger or how they can distract themselves. During the car journey they will be 'on edge', focusing all of their attention either on signs of danger or on trying to desperately take their mind off the danger by distracting themselves (further safety behaviours). As if this was not bad enough, they will then focus on how awful a journey it was once they get home and thus the cycle of worry ahead of the next journey continues.

Table 3 shows an example of Susan's toxic trio in action, which she has recorded on a diary sheet given to her by her CBT Therapist. There is a blank version of this in the appendix for you to use and record your experiences.

Table 3 - The stages of anxiety maintenance

Before the event	During the event	After the event
What I tell myself will happen What I imagine I or the situation will look like The things I do which I believe help me cope	What I say to myself about what is happening Where I place my focus of attention The things I do which I believe keep me safe	What I tell myself about the outcome What parts of the event I recall and focus on How I think this applies to the same situation in the future
SUSAN's EXAMPLE - Driving *"I'm going to crash"* Imagining myself panicky at the wheel of my car or tense and fidgety as a passenger Not thinking about the journey until I'm about to get into the car <u>OR</u> planning what to do or say whilst in the car	*"I'm in danger / I'm too anxious / I can't cope"* Looking out for signs of bad / dangerous driving or hazards Telling the driver about hazards / 'ghost' braking / closing my eyes / holding the seat	*"I was lucky to not be in a crash"* *"It's true the roads are dangerous"* Focusing on 'near misses' Dreading the next journey

As you can see from the diary, Susan was using catastrophic thinking about the outcome of her car journey and believing this thought led to her fight or flight response being triggered. Susan tried to cope with this by either not thinking about the car journey until she was opening the passenger door or she would spend lots of time planning what she would do to keep herself occupied during the journey.

Once in the car and already in threat mode, Susan was scanning the roads for danger and believed that she was keeping herself safe by giving lots of advice to his husband. Susan used safety behaviours such as closing her eyes at roundabouts and gripped the seat tightly.

After the journey was over, Susan did not focus on the fact that she was safe. It felt like she had 'gotten away with it'. Her memory of the journey was of all the near misses and signs of bad driving from others. This led to her dreading the next time she had to travel by car.

Can you see how each stage in this process feeds into the next?

Have a go at writing out your own thoughts and behaviour before, during and after car journeys in the worksheet that is in the appendices.

10. Brain as computer metaphor

Now that you know why you react to things the way you do I am going to introduce you to some powerful techniques to help you minimise the impact your unwanted thoughts and feelings have on your when travelling in a car. This is what I call *achieving control without control*. The less we try to control things that should not and cannot be controlled, the more control we have over how much they affect us.

The theory behind 1-2-3 is based on an idea called competition retrieval and was put forward by Chris Brewin which, in layman's terms suggests that we can have two competing templates in our mind that we use as maps of how ourselves and the world works. These templates could be considered to come from either our primitive brain or our logical brain as described earlier in the book. The template that is reinforced the most is the one that our brain will run automatically. You could think of it like a computer operating system (OS) automatically running Windows or Linux. Often what has happened with clients I see is that either the wrong OS is running as the default software and the competing one needs reactivating or they never really had a competing one in the first place.

Your OS consists of a catalogue of recurring and predictable thoughts, emotions and intentions that influence how you behave. This 'programme' is activated every time you get in a car. If you recall, part of Dave's programme was that he was weak for feeling anxious during car journeys.

Your safety behaviours tends to lead to predictable outcomes (your safety) and these outcomes usually reinforce your recurring thoughts creating a vicious cycle – "I'm only still alive because I gave so and so advice".

These have also been called schemas by other authors and their maintenance called *schema perpetuation*. The schema is perpetuated through the bias that I talked about earlier on.

What this means is that year after year your OS remains the same and you do not switch to another, potentially more effective OS and is illustrated in the diagram below.

Figure 10

Primitive brain installs unhelpful OS

↓

Brain automatically runs this 'fear programme' when you travel in a car

↓

Primitive brain tells you to behave in ways that support the programme (checking for signs of danger / avoiding certain routes

↓

Brain continues to automatically run the 'fear programme' when you travel in a car

In CBT we are in essence trying to deactivate the unhelpful OS (the programme that has been installed by your primitive brain) and reactivate or install the helpful version (developed by the cortex). We do this by giving you competing ways of thinking about car travel and how you feel when you are on the road. We also encourage you to change what you do so that you can learn that you are relatively safe rather than in grave danger.

It will be easier to deactivate the unhelpful one if you already have the competing but dormant version in your locker so to speak but it is possible to have just the one OS installed if this is all you have ever known. If this is the case then self-help alone may not be sufficient to help you de-activate this OS and develop a competing version and therefore you may require additional support from an accredited CBT Therapist after reading this book.

11. Barriers to change

Now that you have learned how your mind works and perhaps what has made you vulnerable to heightened anxiety about car travel, it is time to truly ask yourself whether you are ready to change. You might think *'what's this guy on about? I'm sick of feeling this way of course I am ready to change!*

From my experience of working with hundreds of clients I can tell you that they are all sick and tired of the impact that self-criticism, irritability, sadness, worry, obsessions, shyness and panic have on their lives on a daily basis but not all of them are truly ready to change.

Human beings do not like change. It is often said that we are creatures of habit and following the same routine be it the same job, same relationship, same friends, same hobbies, same tv programmes, is what we like doing best. This is fine if all of these things are working for us but if we are aware that we no longer love our partner, no longer share the same interests with friends, no longer feel challenged at work then we are faced with a very clear albeit difficult choice. Stick with what we know and expect to feel everything that will come with being in a dissatisfying relationship, friendship group, job *or* accept that we need to make some changes and be willing to make room for the discomfort that will naturally occur from shaking up a world that is so familiar to us.

You may have found yourself in a comfort zone where you are able to avoid the anxiety of car travel through limiting your journeys. You may find this an inconvenience but can get by and adapt to walking, cycling or getting public transport.

For you to change your avoidance behaviour, the costs of this need to outweigh the perceived benefits and if this is not the case then you are unlikely to put yourself through the exposure that is needed to overcome your problem.

Avoidance works for people in that it provides short term respite from unwanted thoughts and feelings and it is therefore powerfully reinforcing and difficult to give up. In order to confront your avoidance there needs to be a reward waiting at the other side. In other words, you need to sell change to yourself.

To begin this, I would like you to ask yourself the first two questions and write down as many responses as you can think of in support of each. Once you have this down on paper I would then ask you to consider which you are drawn the most to, on balance. It might be that there are more reasons to change but the couple of reasons not to, outweigh this in your mind. Either way, you are putting on the table all the advantages and all the disadvantages.

Question 1: What do I stand to gain, potentially by changing?

Question 2: What will I lose by changing?

Then….

Question 3: Having considered the pros and cons have you decided to change?

Be honest with yourself about what you might stand to lose from changing. Perhaps life is easier in some ways by keeping things how they are. Perhaps the rewards of change are not important enough to you to make you want to drop avoidance.

If you have decided that change is what you want right now then I have identified what I believe to be the most common obstacles to people following through with change, that is the thoughts they tend to 'fuse with'. Again, I would like you to be honest in your assessment of the obstacle(s) you would most closely identify with. These obstacles mirror the stories that we fuse with which take us in the opposite direction to our values.

Table 4

Typical thoughts that people fuse with	Typical behaviours
It's too hard I'll never be able to do that Other people don't have these struggles I can get by using the bus or walking to places I can't stand these feelings	Putting things off / making excuses Over-thinking and talking themselves out of change Using safety behaviours (insisting others do the driving or only you do, taking diazepam, using alcohol)

One of the greatest hurdles to following through with change for a lot of people is 'riding the storm' of the uncomfortable thoughts and feelings that they experience when starting to change how they live their life.

When we are faced with something we consider to be dangerous our fight or flight response goes off and our bodies sets off a chain of normal reactions to help us deal with the perceived threat. For some people who experience *anxiety sensitivity* the very thought of sitting with these feelings fills them with dread. Anxiety sensitivity means that you have a heightened awareness of subtle changes to unusual but normal physical sensations such as an increase in heart rate, change in breathing, body temperature, gastro-intestinal processes (butterflies in the stomach) which other people would either not notice or would dismiss without further attention. You may also experience these sensations as being more unpleasant than people who I'll call 'distress tolerant'.

In Part 3 I will be introducing you to mindfulness which is very useful for developing skills in distress tolerance.

Part 3

The 1-2-3 way of managing anxious thoughts and feelings about driving and road travel

12. Thoughts are not facts

The first step in de-activating your unhelpful OS is learning to spot the recurring and predictable thoughts which reflect your view of yourself and the world which you recorded on your anxiety equation sheet. This is called 'Theory A'.

Theory A tells you that the roads are dangerous; full of bad drivers and that another accident is highly likely. It might also tell you that you're an unlucky person and more likely to have another accident than other people. Your safety behaviours prevent you from finding out that this may not be totally true and therefore you continue to snack on this mental junk food. Accepting at face value or fusing with Theory A leads to you dreading every car journey and paying lots of attention to signs of bad driving and gives you a strong feeling of impending doom. This creates anxiety and further hypervigilance. You then attribute your survival to the fact that you were on guard and as a result of this, averted danger and therefore Theory A continues to operate.

The way to change how you feel is to understand how Theory A is creating and is exacerbating your own vicious cycle (remember Dave in Part 1). You may be quite aware of the thoughts that pass through your mind when anxious or you may need to develop some skills in identifying thoughts by stopping them in their tracks. This can be easier said than done however with practice you can learn to spot unhelpful thoughts and begin to change your relationship with them.

There are a multitude of ways in which we can put a distance between ourselves and our thoughts. To reference ACT theory, most of us are *fused* with 'the conceptualised self', believing without question the stories that we have carried around about ourselves and others since childhood. Dave's belief that he is a pussy for feeling anxious is an example of stories that the mind stores and reproduces. These are stored in the unhelpful OS and by being lost in this fog of fusion we do not get to step back and take perspective on these stories which reinforce the OS (Theory A).

It can be difficult or scary for individuals such as Dave to entertain the idea of defusing from these stories because they feel familiar and like the truth about how things are. In schema therapy they speak about schemas as entities that fight for survival and that they are highly resistant to change.

Dave was initially quite reluctant to see anxiety as anything other than a sign of weakness however when his therapist suggested that they ask other people what they think about the meaning of feeling anxious, this led to a shift in Dave's attitude. He learned from the survey responses that people see anxiety as part and parcel of difficult life experiences and that even 'strong' people have these physical sensations in situations they see as threatening.

I want you to notice the resistance that emerges in you when you try to challenge your own beliefs about your thoughts, emotions or physical sensation or when you try to change how you behave in certain situations.

Developing meta-cognitive awareness

Meta-cognition is a term I introduced in Part One and if you remember, this means thinking about thinking and this is absolutely crucial when it comes to breaking vicious cycles involving unhelpful thoughts.

In everyday life, people talk about having a devil on one shoulder and an angel on the other, usually when referring to them trying to be 'good' and avoid certain temptations such as eating 'naughty' food when they are dieting. Without necessarily recognising it, people are putting a distance between themselves and their thoughts by assigning characters that play out predictable messages to them or push them in to certain behaviours. This is a rudimentary form of defusion.

How to defuse

Fusing with these repetitive stories is like snacking on mental junk food, it feels so good and right because it is familiar yet you don't always see the damage that it is doing until it is too late. The first step in defusion is to take a step back and notice the stories, label them and how frequently they are occurring. Initially we need to create some doubt about how true these thoughts are. We do this by proposing an alternative OS or belief system which we will call Theory B.

Now here's the thing – there will always be a shred of truth to any negative thought. There is always the chance that something bad will happen, that another person may dislike us, that we made a mistake but the difference here is that negative thoughts are out of proportion. If you remember, in Cognitive Therapy there is a list of thinking errors that we can make reference to and check out whether our thoughts fall under one or more of these categories.

Question to ask myself

What tells me these thoughts are not entirely true?

Would I recommend this way if thinking to another person?

(often we say horrible things about ourselves or the world but would not dream of doing so to a friend or family member. Why should we be any different?)

Constructing Theory B

I am going to presume that you have little idea of what Theory B might consist of at this moment in time and consequently I am going to make a suggestion as to what it might sound like.

Theory B is along the lines of.........

I am no more likely to be involved in another accident than anyone else therefore I do not need to take any more precautions than the average person does

I want you to rate how much you instinctively believe theory B from 0-100 with zero being 'don't believe it at all' and a hundred being completely convinced that it is true.

Theory A v Theory B

Everything that you will be doing from now on as a passenger or car driver will be to gather evidence to support Theory B and undermine Theory A. Remember, Theory A only gives us the illusion of total safety. Theory B is the competing OS that we are going to install so that your brain has the option of running this programme when you are in a car. Your positive experiences of car travel log can be used as evidence to support Theory B.

Consequences of fusing with what our mind tells us

You may have been having these stories go round and round in your mind for years, decades even prior to the accident. They are a well trodden path and therefore can be difficult to defuse from. I would like you to consider the consequence of continuing to fuse with these stories so that you are able to see the cost of staying hooked.

Dave's consequences were that he and Mel regularly bickered and their relationship was strained. He remained anxious and fearful and his confidence as a driver remained low.

Susan's consequences were that she had to turn down job opportunities because she could not bring herself to travel further than short journeys around the village where she lived.

Ask yourself the set of questions below for each of the stories that you have identified.

What is the interpersonal consequence of continuing to fuse with this story? (what effect does it have on my relationships?)

What is the emotional consequence of continuing to fuse with this story? (what feelings keep showing up?)

What is the cognitive consequence of continuing to fuse with this story? (how does this affect my confidence / the way I think about others and the future?)

Creating a persona

Practicing defusion helps to improve our meta-cognitive awareness and giving anxious thoughts a persona is also a very visual way of separating you from your primitive brain thoughts. Many types of therapy use personas to achieve this distancing. Steve Peters uses 'The Chimp' in his mind management model, Jeffrey Young uses 'modes' in schema Therapy where there are similarities to Eric Berne's Parent, Adult and Child ego states in Transactional Analysis. In Cognitive Therapy, there is the concept of a bully (in OCD) and a poisoned parrot (when conceptualising self-criticism).

Creating the distance and gaining some objectivity is step one, defusing from the persona is step two and perhaps the more difficult part. Whilst we might be able to give, for example our anxious thoughts the persona of ourselves when we were a child we might still be so fused with these thoughts that we continue to agree with what this person is saying.

There is the capacity in all of us to take a step back from our child 'mode' and view the world from our adult perspective. The adult recognizes that the world is not risk free yet in spite of this, would wish to bring joy into your life. The child persona in your mind only wishes to focus on what could go wrong. When we can begin to recognize that these personas are not 'us' we can begin to separate in our mind the things that represent us and those which represent the aims of the persona. We can comfort our child mode by explaining the way the world is but also providing comfort and understanding.

The simplest way to make this division is to think that anything which relates to your values is *you* and most of the thoughts that relate to fear are the priorities of the *primitive brain and the child persona.*

Here are some ideas for how you might create this distance between you and the persona.

Worksheet 5

Who does this persona remind me of? (a parent / family member / your anxious child 'self')

_____

What does this persona look like? (is it human form / animal / supernatural)

_____

What does it sound like?

_____

What might I say to this persona to help reason with it / calm it down / nurture it?

_____

Once you have constructed the image of the persona you can then imagine that whenever you experience car travel worries that they belong to them and not you.

Susan thought that her persona reminded her of when she was a little girl. Susan decided that she would try to comfort her child self and 'tell her how it is'. First of all, Susan listened to the concerns of her younger self and wrote down all of her worries. After this, Susan explained to herself that it was understandable to have these fears but then emphasized what they would be missing out on by continuing to avoid certain situations. Susan reminded her child self of all the times she has coped with more stressful and dangerous life events and committed to riding out any anxious feelings during car journeys.

I will be helping you consider the things which make you 'you' in the section on values and once you have clarified your values you will be in a better position to see the contrast with the persona and what it represents.

Labelling the story

There is a certain predictability to our thoughts for example if I said to you – Mary had a little……you would probably think lamb, however, maybe I was going to say Mary had a little cut on her thumb. The point here is that our brain is very predictable and jumps to conclusions.

To begin to 'spot the story' I always ask clients to picture a carousel and get them to consider that their minds produce the same variations of specific stories that go round and round like a carousel.

Common stories that we fuse with can be divided into themes about the self, the world and the future in keeping with Aaron Beck's Negative cognitive triad and I have listed some examples below.

<u>Stories about the self</u>

The "I'm unlucky" story
The 'I can't cope' story
The 'I'm an anxious person' story

Stories about the world
The "road is full of idiot drivers" story
The "roads are not safe…" story
The "it's bound to happen again" story

Stories about the future
The "I'll never get better" story
The 'I'm ill" story
The "I'm still in danger" story

Can you think of any that apply to you or any not listed here?

When you try to DEFUSE – that is, observe what your mind tells you about doing this exercise, your mind will try to resist this. Here are some of my predictions about the types of things your mind will say to you about it.

"It's alright for him to do this, he hasn't got anxiety problems like me"

"What's all this hippie shit, it won't make a difference"

"The roads are still dangerous, looking at good driving won't change that"

Do you identify with any of these? If so, that is to be expected, that is what your brain does, especially when you are in a threat-focused mindset you will be having lots and lots of negative thoughts that if you fuse with, will increase your anxiety even further and pull you away from activities linked to your values.

Have a go at identifying the stories you think your mind produces about self, world and future below.

Stories my mind tells me about 'myself'

Stories my mind tells me about the world

Stories my mind tells me about the future

Summary of the techniques and of my learning

1. Noticing the story and its origins – when do I first recall thinking that and who does it remind me of? Perhaps a family member was always talking about bad drivers or lack of safety on the roads when you were growing up

_____

2. Noticing what's wrong with the story – is it full of thinking errors? Is it a long time since the belief was tested? Changing our response to the story by picturing the mental carousel (same stories going round and round)

_____

3. Name the story, consider the consequences of fusing with it and pick a defusion method that appeals to you.

_____

Now that you are able to take a step back from your thoughts, I want to show you in the next chapter how to deal with the unwanted physical sensations and emotions that show up for you when you travel by car.

We will begin to look at building on your meta-cognitive awareness by learning some basic mindfulness skills.

13. Changing how we respond to our feelings

If our primitive brain is here to stay then surely the answer is to learn how to judge when we are in real danger and when we are *perceiving danger* because if we are really under threat then we want our primitive brain to 'kick in' and help us survive. If we are perceiving danger that is not really there then we want to be able to calm our primitive brain down not cut it out altogether.
Remember what I said about having your cake and eating it – you can't have both – being totally safe and living a rich and meaningful life, there will always be a trade off.

Unlike reading, writing and arithmetic, no one formally teaches us how to recognize different emotions never mind deal with them. We are expected to know what we are feeling, why we are feeling it and to be able to deal with it. The chances are that you learned how to cope with life's ups and downs by observing your parents responses (or other main caretakers if they were absent). In psychology this is called *modelling*.

The fortunate ones learn through observing their parents healthy reactions to emotions, the skills of labeling emotions and responding to them flexibly. They learn to differentiate emotions, to appreciate that they will pass and therefore do not view them as intolerable. They use a range of emotional regulation strategies such as talking to friends, exercise, relaxation and problem solving.

If you struggle to tolerate high levels of emotion then perhaps certain emotions were not expressed in the family unit or you got the impression that you had to be 'strong' and not show any sign of perceived weakness.

It could simply be that you have found that avoidance is a very successful way of blocking unwanted thoughts and feelings and this has becomes your default way of responding to the world around you.

I noticed this *distress intolerance* in a significant proportion of clients that I worked with early on in my career as a therapist when trying to use a purely CT approach.
Clients would tell me that they understood the benefits of thinking and behaving differently but they either didn't believe the more rational thoughts or they found encountering anxiety provoking situations to be too distressing.

Fortunately, offshoots of CT like ACT and CFT came along and bridged this gap by explaining why we find it hard to think differently and why some people struggle to tolerate their feelings more than others. The wisdom of these therapies and techniques I applied helped me plug this therapeutic gap and I will be sharing this pooled wisdom with you by introducing you to methods drawn from both of these approaches throughout the book.

Emotional literacy

Developing emotional literacy means identifying the specific emotion or emotions that you are experiencing at any given time. We can use mindfulness practices to increase our emotional literacy and I will be showing you an example of how to do this later in this chapter.

The first stage of emotional literacy is to learn about some of the main emotions that you have been trying to block, after all the more we know the better equipped we are to deal with them. These emotions produce clean discomfort in us yet if we battle with them they become greater than they need to be and the dirty discomfort is born as illustrated previously in Figure 7.

It is vital that you put some time in to prepare for how you plan to substitute the strategies you currently use and anticipate reasons that your mind will give you about why you can't or shouldn't change. I would suggest picking a specific day or date to implement small changes and then reflect on the success and challenges of making the changes and gradually build from there, increasing the frequency of the healthier emotional regulation strategies.

Using mindfulness to enhance meta-cognitive awareness

To be mindful is simply to be fully focused on whatever we are doing in the present moment. This is harder than it sounds because most of the time your mind is trying to drag you off into the past "Why did I do this / why didn't I do that?" or into the future "What if this happens/ what if that happens".

When we learn to be mindful we recognise and label these processes "Now I am ruminating" or "Now I am worrying". We can decide whether we want to continue with them or let them go and focus on the things we can do something about in the present moment.

Sitting with your emotions, as opposed to running a mile from them might be a very alien concept to you as it is to most of us and especially Dave who had distress intolerance around his heart racing in the car. Nevertheless, Dave was encouraged by his therapist to try the mindfulness exercise in Figure 11. I want you to have a go at this emotional regulation strategy by making some room for the emotions that you normally avoid or block when they arise during car journeys. I am going to introduce you to a mindfulness exercise that with practice, will allow to you to develop a much healthier relationship with your feelings and your thoughts. This can be practiced outside of the car, in your everyday life and the more often you practice mindfulness, the more proficient you will become at it.

One way to think of anxious thoughts, emotions and physical sensations is the tin can monster. This is a technique used in ACT and in this example something that seems overwhelming and scary like anxiety, we can break down into its component parts. You can do this within the space of five minutes or so with your eyes open or closed. In the following exercise, you will be using defusion skills learned in the previous section as part of this mindfulness practice.

Figure 11 - Example mindfulness script for driving or travelling as a car passenger

I want you to imagine that your attention is like a camera and at present it is on a panoramic view, taking in everything around you. Just take a moment to be aware of all the things in the environment that is going on. Notice the sound of traffic, notice your temperature, notice what your feet feel like against the floor and how it feels to be sat on the seat. Notice anything that you can smell.

Now I want you to zoom that camera in so that the focus of your attention is on your breath. You are not trying to control your breath in any way, just bring your awareness to the experience. Notice where the breath begins and ends. It may help to close your eyes at this point. Does it start in your nostrils or your mouth? Follow its journey. Does it go down into your chest or your stomach?

At this point you may notice that something else is trying to pull your attention away from the breath. It could be your thoughts, it could be sounds that you can hear, it could be a physical sensation in your body.

I want you to just notice this and guide your attention back on to your breathing. If you have to do this many times during the exercise, that is ok. <u>The skill is in noticing when the mind has wandered not in preventing it from wandering.</u>

Your breath is your anchor to the present moment. Too often our mind is in the past or the future. All we can influence is now. If your mind starts taking you to imaginary scenarios of a car crash then you can use the breath as a way of anchoring your attention in the here and now.

Next, I want you to notice what thoughts are passing through your mind. I don't want you to challenge these thoughts or to make them go away. I want you to be curious about what your mind is telling you right now. Perhaps it is making judgments about this exercise? "This is boring" "This is stupid" "This is unpleasant" are typical thoughts our mind produces. By noticing these thoughts as just products of our mind we are de-fused from them. If we get caught up in listening to them and obeying them or trying to argue against them, we become fused with their content.

The anxiety that you feel about getting in a car is like a tin can monster. It looks big and scary at first glance yet when we look at it more closely, we can see that it is made up of bits of string and tin cans. Some of the cans are the thoughts that you have when you think about being in a car or that you have whilst travelling. As you sit in the car now, I want you to notice the thoughts you are having about being there.

I want you to simply allow those thoughts to be there and acknowledge that this is just your primitive brain sending out a warning because it is trying to protect you. By recognizing this, we can acknowledge but then let these thoughts go.

I want you expand your awareness to the other 'tin cans', that is, any emotions that you are experiencing right now. If it is boredom, what does this feel like in your body? If it is anxiety, whereabouts do you experience that? Is it in your stomach, your chest, your shoulders? Zoom your camera in further. It can be useful to give this sensation a shape and a colour.

You can breathe into this area, imagine that you are channelling a soothing breath into that area of discomfort or tension. You are not removing the feeling by doing this but containing it.

Open your eyes and expand your awareness back to your environment. Take in the sights, the sounds, the smell. Try to let that spirit of observation stay with you. Be curious about what thoughts will arise during your car journey. If a strong physical feeling shows up, zoom your attention in on. Breath into it.

It might be helpful to practice this in the comfort of your own home for the first time so that you 'get the gist' of mindfulness before trying it out in the car.

Myths about mindfulness before we get started

Whilst mindfulness appears to be en vogue there are several common myths about it which I would like to address first and foremost. The most common misconception is that to be mindful is to have a completely still and clear mind. This is not possible due to how our brains naturally work. The primitive brain never shuts off because it is always looking out for us for survival purposes. The skill is in noticing when our mind wanders or is hijacked by the primitive brain and then guiding our attention back, not in preventing our mind from wandering.

Common excuses for not being mindful

I don't have time
It's not for me, its for hippy types
I've tried it and I can't clear my mind

If this sounds like you then please just give it a go. You can do mindfulness in minutes and remember the skill is noticing not stopping thoughts.

14. Identifying your values and making changes

Now that you have learned how to spot and defuse the recurring stories that your mind throws at you in car travel situations and how to contain uncomfortable feelings that arise, I want you to think very thoroughly about the kind of life you want. Up until now you have been *consumed by what you don't want*. With this shift in perspective we are now focusing on committing to pursuing our values <u>despite</u> what thoughts and feelings show up along the way.

What are values?

Moving towards a life that you want involves getting in touch with your values and in doing so will often involve difficult decisions that will have an effect on other people (examples - leaving a relationship that is unfulfilling, the uncertainty of changing job, meeting new people socially).
It is very easy to be consumed with thinking about what you no longer want in your life, however feeling better does not occur in a vacuum, by this I mean we need to start laying the foundations for the life we want INSTEAD of what we have at present. This echoes the principle laid down in Part One of the book, about *accepting* what it is to be human and the things we cannot change or escape from and then channelling our energies into creating the conditions for leading the life we want.

Values are the things that matter to us and they are like compass points. A life without values is like a ship without a compass. When the inevitable strong winds or storms that life throws at us arise we get blown off course.

If we have clear compass points then we can redirect ourselves once the storm has passed. If we have no direction that is when we drift whichever way the tide takes us, often further away from being the person who we want to be.

An important caveat here is that there are no guarantees. We are not guaranteed to be 100% safe on the roads simply by thinking less negatively or pursuing our goals, again, coming back to acceptance, *uncertainty and adversity are part and parcel of being human.* This might sound obvious but most of us have a hard time truly accepting this.

What is a guarantee is that if we continue to do what we have always done (avoid, ruminate, let ourselves be bullied by our anxious thoughts) we will continue to stuck with a restricted life and with the feeling that good things are what happen to other people and not us.

Identifying values

Identifying your values is not about planning every minute detail but about getting in touch with what is important to you and what would give your life meaning. The main question I want you to consider is this.

If you weren't trying to avoid certain thoughts and feelings what would you be doing in these key domains of your life?

I also want you to consider what is more important to you – your value or your illusion of total safety.

Family and relationships

What kind of partner / parent / son/ daughter / friend do I want to be and how close a match is my current behaviour?

Leisure and Travel

Where do I want to go to – am I an explorer or am I happy just to stick to what I know

Work and learning

What sort of job do I want and where would I need to travel to for this?

What things do I want to study / learn more about? Where will I need to go to do this?

Examples – Relationships and Work

Dave wanted to be a spontaneous partner who could go away on surprise romantic weekends at the drop of a hat. Unfortunately this would mean driving on the motorway and therefore his current avoidance behaviour meant that he was not living his life in keeping with this value.

Susan wanted to work in the city as there were more career prospects in comparison to her home town. Unfortunately this would mean travelling on roads with higher speed limits and therefore her current avoidance behaviour meant that she was not living her life in keeping with this value.

Worksheet 6 - Excerpt from Dave's Values Assessment

Life domain	What is important to me	Thoughts I fuse with/avoid & feelings that I avoid and which prevent me from valued living
Romantic relationship	To be spontaneous and to keep things fresh and exciting	*"The motorway is dangerous"* Anxiety

Setting goals to move in the direction of your values

Without goals our life can lack meaning and direction. When you are thinking about your values it is useful to link specific goals to each of them and these become your targets that you are working towards every time you approach rather than avoid driving situations.

An example of this is Motorway driving for Dave who decided that......

Despite feeling nervous and fearing another accident I will begin to drive a few junctions on my nearest motorway because this goal is in keeping with my value of staying in touch with my family regularly and of exploring the country.

Remember there will always be a tradeoff between what Dave wants and what his caveman brain wants.
Dave has decided that the value of staying in touch with his family *outweighs* the risk he is taking of driving on the motorway. By avoiding this journey, Dave would feel safer in the short term but he would not be living his life in keeping with his values.

Once you have clarified your goals and their respective values I want you to come up with a plan of how you intend to reclaim your life by exposing yourself to being a passenger or driver on a more frequent basis.

How to set up your recovery plan

Rather than throwing yourself in at the deep end and trying to conquer your most anxiety provoking journey or approaching exposure in a haphazard fashion, it can be useful to create a hierarchy. A hierarchy can be thought of as a ladder in which you start on the bottom rungs and gradually climb higher.

A hierarchy is a great way of focusing you on where you want to get to at the end your exposures. If you find that some exposures are easier than you predicted then you can move higher up the ladder so to speak. You do not need to work through a hierarchy slowly and sequentially. Starting small is about giving you some confidence. You can write one out like Dave's just using a blank sheet of A4 paper.

Figure 12 - Dave's hierarchy

Drive to work on the motorway once a week

Drive for three hours to see family on the motorway

Drive for an hour on the motorway

Drive three junctions on the motorway

Drive one junction on the motorway

Travel as a passenger for an hour on the motorway

Travel as a passenger for three junctions on the motorway

Travel as a passenger for one junction on the motorway

Working all of the way through your hierarchy might take months, even a couple of years so it can be helpful to set short term, medium term and long term goals which will move you in the direction of your values.

Dave set these goals which he broke down into what he would like to be doing within the next couple of week, months and by the end of the year.

Short term – To stop giving Mel advice about how to drive when I'm travelling as a passenger in the car

Medium term – To drive one junction on the motorway

Long term – To start driving to work and back again on the motor way network
Susan's goals were

Short term – To drop the grandchildren off at school in my car one morning next week

Medium term – To drive on a road where the speed limit is above 30 mph

Long term – To pick the grandchildren up again every Friday and drive on 50 mph roads to meet up with friends for lunch

You can see that the goals are fairly specific rather than vague. By setting specific goals you can 'tick off' when you have reached them and you can also measure your progress more effectively.

I would like you to list the things that you are going to aim to do whilst reading this book

My short term goals

My medium term goals

My long term goals

Getting the most from exposure

There are several golden rules when it comes to establishing an exposure hierarchy. The first is that you need to be consistent – there is little point in using safety behaviours on some journeys and not others. Your primitive brain needs sufficient evidence of your relative safety in order to be satisfied that it can turn the alarm off. This requires a consistent approach to car travel.

The second golden rule is that you need to carry out exposure frequently. If you only get in the car once a month then this is not frequent enough for learning and a change of perspective to take place.

So that you are able to see that your anxiety level will reduce with time and repeated exposures it is useful to record your Subjective Units of Distress (SUDS) just before you get in the car, at regular intervals during and at the end.

Checking your SUDS is like carrying an emotional thermometer around with you. This helps you to see your anxiety as a sliding scale rather than being calm or terrified with no in between.

Susan rated her SUDS as 60/100 when she was approaching the car, 70 once the car set off and it went up to 90 when she approached a busy roundabout. Susan noticed that her SUDS reduced to 40 by the end of the thirty minute journey. The next time she was about to get in the car her SUDS were 50, 65 at departure and only 75 at the roundabout. It also took less time for Susan's SUDS to fall to 40 with a rating of 20 by the end of this journey.

It is more important to reflect on what you have discovered from your car journey than how much your SUDS reduce by. Some people experience a rapid reduction in SUDS ratings through exposure whilst others do not. It is also important that the reason your SUDS reduce is not down to you using safety behaviours as this will affect your learning and reinforces Theory A.

Table 5 provides a summary of the best way to carry out your exposures.

Table 5 - Helpful and unhelpful ways to carry out exposure tasks

Helpful	Unhelpful
<ul><li>Plan to carry out specific exposures on specific days at specific times</li><li>Taking time to sit down and write some notes about what you have learned from doing each exposure including the changes in SUDS ratings</li><li>Reminding yourself before each exposure what it is that you are trying to test out and using mindfulness to monitor your urges to carry out safety behaviours</li></ul>	<ul><li>Only carrying out the exposure when I feel in the mood for it</li><li>Carrying out the exposure by chance and not planning or reflecting on the experience</li><li>Trying not to think about it until you are getting in the car and then hoping for the best OR trying to get it over and done with as quickly as possible</li></ul>

Section Summary

1. Commit to increasing your psychological flexibility by accepting the inevitable emotional pain (clean discomfort) and adverse life events that arise from our time on this planet. Remember, acceptance is not the same as resigning yourself to the status quo. Acceptance is about recognition of what we cannot change (our primitive brain and its functions) and committing to building a life that we do have a say over. Acceptance is acknowledging the field of nettles but seeking out the roses by clearing what path we can through the nettles.

2. Make room for uncomfortable driving-related thoughts and feelings through defusion and mindfulness and in doing so you are building resilience. We also become more emotionally literate this way and are able to handle even the most difficult of experiences in time

3. Get in touch with your values and commit to living your life based on these values rather than on your current mood state or being based around avoiding the things that upset you. A life without values is like a ship without a compass, when the inevitable strong winds or storms that life throws at us arise we get blown off course. If we have clear compass points then we can redirect ourselves once the storm has passed. If we have no direction that is when we drift whichever way the tide takes us, often further away from being the person who we want to be.

Part 4 - Maintaining your progress

15. Building on what you already learned

Now that you have had some experience of exposure to your previously avoided car journeys it is important that you continue to put into practice what you have learned from your exposures.

You will have begun to test out which theory holds most weight – Theory A or Theory B by travelling or driving progressively further distances as you look to return to pre-accident functioning. It might be tempting to stop at this point and be satisfied with moderate progress whereby you are travelling again on some roads or a few junctions of a motorway however this would be extremely short sighted.

It is absolutely imperative that you maintain the momentum you have built up by continuing to put yourself in situations that you have been avoiding. I often use the example of a snowball rolling down a hill. The longer it goes the faster it goes and the bigger it gets. This applies to your motivation and the evidence that you are compiling for Theory B.
You need to build up lots of evidence for Theory B and it often takes hundreds of journeys to switch the OS that is running in the hippocampus from the unhelpful to the helpful version. For that reason, it is very useful to keep written evidence of your progress so that you can see how your anxiety ratings and belief ratings have changed over time. The worksheets you have used already can be photocopied to use again and again until you reach a point where your anxiety is minimal.

To draw together your new way of thinking about and behaving during car journeys I would like you to fill out the sheet below (a copy of which can be found in the appendix) which is the helpful alternative to the toxic trio of anxiety maintenance which we looked at in Chapter 9. Susan came up with the following alternatives to say to herself and do before, during and after every car journey.

Worksheet 7 - The stages of anxiety reversal

Before the event	During the event	After the event
Alternative thoughts and behaviours	**Alternative thoughts and behaviours**	**Alternative thoughts and behaviours**
Remind myself of how many car journeys I have had that have been safe Consider what safety behaviours I will be tempted to use in the car and plan for where I will place my focus of attention instead	Rate my anxiety out of 100 and watch it rise and gradually fall without having to do anything to make this happen Place my attention on signs of good driving and non-threatening stimuli	Reflect on what happened to my anxiety level, how well I coped without my safety behaviours Consider what I have learned from dropping my safety behaviours. I didn't crash yet I didn't avoid certain routes – what does this tell me about how much danger I am in?

Using flashcards to cement Theory B in your mind

If you find that some car journeys are trickier to handle than others even after you have used the anxiety reversal worksheet then flashcards can help jog your memory about what it is you are trying to think and do differently whilst in the car. They are visual prompts and are a very useful way to remind yourself of what Theory B consists of when you are sat in the car. Theory A does not disappear – we can only 'de-activate it' and therefore under certain conditions the thoughts and behaviours associated with Theory A will come back, sometimes when you least expect them to.

Flashcards can be carried around in your wallet or purse or you could have an electronic version by storing some prompts in the notes app on your mobile phone.

A flashcard should be concise and only about the size of a credit card, containing a few statements to prompt you into thinking and behaving in keeping with Theory B. It might also say something about the urges and anxious thoughts that might arise and how you plan to answer them back.

Figure 13 - Example of flashcards created by Susan

When I get in the car I will be tempted to sit in the back seat and to give my husband Ron constant updates about hazards that I can see out of the window. These are my safety behaviours which make me feel safe in the short term but prevent me from learning that I can trust Ron's judgment to keep us safe.

> I can learn to live with the uncertainty of whether or not another accident will occur. The accident I was in did not occur because I was not vigilant enough. It was just one of those things.
>
> I can remind myself of all the accident free journeys I've had since starting therapy and since dropping my safety behaviours.
>
> I will dare myself to sit in the front seat and to pay attention to non-threatening things during the drive such as the scenery or engage in a conversation with Ron

As you can see from the example, Susan is anticipating what she is likely to have the urge to do (sit in the back rather than the front which her primitive brain has told her is dangerous). Susan is also reminding herself of how her healthy adult self views road travel – that there is no certainty but based on the number of journeys she has had, it is a fairly safe form of transport. Susan then gives herself an instruction of what to do instead of going with what her primitive brain wants.

Look how far you have come

I want to remind you that you have learned to see anxiety as an equation, maintained by four separate but interacting variables consisting of how likely you believe another accident is, how bad you predict it would be and whether you think you could cope or be helped by anyone.

Understanding which parts of the equation are the most relevant to you will help you pick out the interventions to help you move forward with your life.

You have also learned that the responses in your mind and body are normal and that it is how we react to our responses that determines how we feel ultimately. The clean discomfort that we feel in situations that could be dangerous is turned into dirty discomfort when we try and fight these feelings or spend too long trying to find a reason for why they have emerged.

Finally you have learned about the types of thoughts which fuel your anxiety and ways to challenge unhelpful patterns of relating to your thinking and you have learned how to contain strong emotional reactions that arise when you set about getting back in the car without your safety behaviours.

1-2-3 Treatment Plan summary

Both Dave and Susan learned how their brain processes traumatic events and how their primitive brain in particular shouts very loudly and makes them focus all of their attention on signs of danger whilst in the car. They learned to separate their thoughts and values from that of their primitive brain which is only interested in their survival, not their happiness.

They also learned some techniques for identifying anxiety provoking thoughts and for dealing with strong physical sensations that emerged when they travelled by car. Dave and Susan identified their values and realized that their drive to stay safe was vastly overshadowing their drive to live a full and meaningful life and this led them to reconsider their levels of avoidance.

16. Relapse Prevention

Developing the art of reflection

Whether I am working with depressed or anxious clients, one of my main goals is to help them increase or develop an ability to reflect on the consequences of what they think and what they do but also on what they learn from responding differently to the situations they are in. The skill of reflection becomes a lifelong process which helps to improve their capacity to take a step back from stresses in their lives and to examine how effective their ways of coping really are.

Reflecting on your progress will be about relating your new experiences back to Theory A and Theory B and looking at which one appears to be supported the most. You need to be mindful here of the tendency to use schemas bias (remember Figure 6) and only filter in negative experiences. It is worth bearing in mind that there will always be near misses on the road and there will always be evidence of bad driving however it is what we make of this that determines the importance to your life.

Anticipating your banana skins

At this stage you might have made some good progress with returning to driving previously avoided routes or increasing your frequency travelling as a car passenger. It might even feel like you are responding automatically in a different way to car journeys, no longer needing to use diaries or your flashcard and this is when you can become complacent. Before we end a course of therapy, I always ask my clients to anticipate what they could slip up on in the future – their banana skins.

Examples of banana skins to watch out for:

❖ You are involved in one or several 'near misses' which are a normal part of driving but which tell your primitive brain that you are in danger.

❖ You witness another road traffic accident and start to believe that you will be next

❖ You attempt an exposure and feel very anxious whilst doing it and you turn the car around and head home

If one of these situations arises it is vitally important that you remind yourself of what Theory B tells us about car travel and that setbacks are common, it is how we respond to them that determine whether we learn from the experience or revert to old habits.

What you tell yourself about 'near misses'

I can guarantee you that during your exposures you will encounter driving situations that fall under the category of 'near misses'. Often this can lead to a temporary setback because people with car travel anxiety take this as evidence in support of Theory A.
One way of countering this is to see near misses as a driving phenomenon in their own right as illustrated by the continuum below

Safe journeys   **Near Misses**   **Accidents**

From this perspective, near misses do not indicate an accident nor do they indicate total safety, instead they represent a normal part of driving.

The traffic light system

Aptly named perhaps, I use the traffic light system as a way of getting people to gauge where they are at with their thinking and behaviour around car travel.

Green tells you that you can carry on as you are. You are thinking about car travel in a balanced way, accepting uncertainty and risk and living your life in keeping with your values. You take reasonable precautions as a driver and passenger without being preoccupied with having a crash.

Amber tells you that perhaps you are starting to slip into old ways of thinking about car travel and that some safety behaviours might have crept back into your journeys. At this point you can take a step back, recognize what is happening and use what you have learned to make the necessary adjustments to your thoughts and behaviour.

Red tells you that you are back to square one, making catastrophic predictions about every car journey, avoiding certain routes and using lots of safety behaviours. If you have reached this point then you will need to revisit everything that has been discussed in this book. You will need to be systematic about reintroducing yourself to regular car journeys without the use of your safety behaviours. It might be that you need to seek help from a suitably qualified and experienced CBT Therapist.

Putting it all together

So far you have learned how your brain works in terms of how it responds to perceived threats by triggering a series of reactions in our body. This puts our brain at odds with itself because the two key parts of the brain have conflicting needs. The primitive brain wants to do everything in it's power to keep us safe and is therefore not interested in our happiness whilst the logical brain wants us to pursue activities that are meaningful to us and will enrich our lives even if this means taking some risks. In essence, you cannot 'have your cake and eat it'. If you want a full and meaningful life then you need to take some risks and accept that sometimes these gambles will pay off and sometimes they won't. If you want to play it safe all the time then you need to accept that you will most likeably be unhappy through a lack of fulfillment.

Summary

1. You have learned how to recognise when the internal conflict is occurring and to take a step back from primitive brain thinking using mindfulness skills and cognitive restructuring.

2. You have also identified your own 'Achilles heel' – the characteristics that make you vulnerable to car travel anxiety and you have had the opportunity to evaluate how useful holding on to these characteristics is and you have a competing way of viewing yourself and others that will be guided by your values.

3. Finally, you have learned what thinking patterns and behaviours keep your problems going and how to reverse them.

17. Information for partners or family members

It is of great importance that when you are being supported by a family member or friend that they help to challenge your old ways of thinking and behaving, not reinforce them.

Often with good intentions, family members, partners and friends can without knowing it, reinforce phobic behaviour by acting as *safety signals* for the person and engage in behaviours that collude with avoidance. An example of this might be to offer to do the driving or to avoid travelling on certain roads with them. Whilst doing this comforts the person in the short term, it prevents them from learning that their fears are often unfounded or at least exaggerated.

Here are some tips for supporting someone doing exposure therapy:

- ✓ Take an interest in their exposure ladder, helping them plan and organise when and where exposures can take place between therapy sessions and once therapy has concluded.

- ✓ Praise them for approach behaviour (when they stay in the situation) or offer encouragement to try again if an exposure is unsuccessful

- ✓ Consider your own behaviour when the person is exposed to the feared object or situation. What can you stop doing that might be feeding their phobia?

- ✓ Explain to them the reasons why you will be withdrawing from acting as a safety signal but make it clear that you are supporting them by doing this and that you would not be helping them overcome their phobia if you remain a safety signal

18. Troubleshooting

Q   I have tried your methods and I still feel anxious when I am in the car

Q   But I still could be in another accident. I need to make sure that I am as safe as possible.

A   Despite understanding the rationale for treatment, clients often default to their tried and tested ways of thinking about the world or with coping with difficult thoughts and feelings through thought suppression, distraction, experiential and behavioural avoidance. There are a few questions below to ask yourself and picking out which one fits with you is likely to help you find the blockage in being where you want to be.

1. Is there a story that you are still fused with? If so, what are the pros and cons of continuing to fuse?

2. Are there certain emotions that you still try to avoid or block?

3. Have you done a values assessment and taken steps to move in the direction of these values?

It is of vital importance that you make mindful attention as much a part of your road travel as brushing your teeth or getting dressed in the morning. I like to use the analogy that if you went to the gym for three months and lost weight, you would need to keep going otherwise the weight will go back on. It is exactly the same with building your mental fitness – if you don't use it, you lose it.

Be honest with yourself about the excuses your mind will generate about why you don't have time to be mindful or why it won't help or why you can't act in accordance with your values.

It is my firm belief that if you have read and taken on board the ideas in this book (including the troubleshooting) and committed to making important changes to your behaviour then you will be well on the way to setting yourself free from car travel anxiety.

I wish you well for the future

Jason

Glossary

Clean discomfort – these are the normal reactions in our body to situations that might be perceived as dangerous to us in some way. Racing thoughts, a pounding heart, increased breathing rate are all forms of 'clean discomfort'

Defusion – Taking a step back from our thoughts and seeing them for what they are – mental events. When we are defused, we decide which thoughts to agree with and which to dismiss

Dirty discomfort – dirty discomfort arises when we try to reason with or make our clean discomfort go away. The feelings in our body or unwanted thoughts are intensified and stick around longer through our unwillingness to have them

Distress Tolerance – The capacity to fully experience and tolerate the full range of human emotions without distraction, avoidance or numbing

Fusion – this occurs when we are our thoughts and we treat all thoughts as important. When we are fused with unhelpful thoughts we are unable to see any other perspective

Rumination – a mental activity whereby you try to search for the reasons for why you feel low and in doing so you withdraw from activities that will make you feel better

SUDS – stands for subjective units of distress and is a scale of 0-100 to help you rate the intensity of any given emotion.

Unintended consequences – the effect of your efforts to protect yourself from a perceived external threat (a place or person) OR internal threat (unwanted thought, emotion or physical sensation)

Values – the things that matter the most to you in your relationships, work, leisure. Your values tell you what kind of person you want to be and what you want to stand for. Goals help you move in the direction of these values.

Willingness – refers to how committed you are to pursuing things that are meaningful to you despite what thoughts, emotions or physical sensations might show up along the way

Worry – a mental activity that involves thinking about a problem without ever arriving at a solution or only thinking about a problem up to a certain point. Worry is different from rumination as it is about the future and is different from problem solving because solutions are not arrived at

APPENDIX SELF HELP / THERAPY WORKSHEETS

Worksheet 1 - Positive Experiences of Driving Log

Day and time	Driving situation	Observations

Worksheet 2

Things I have done to rid myself of accident related thoughts, emotions and physical sensations	How long it worked for ____ days / weeks / months
1. Antidepressant medication 2. Avoiding places or people that trigger certain thoughts 3. Tried to distract myself 4. Tried to or contemplated killing myself 5. Insisted on family members or friends always being round me	

Table 2 – Common errors in thinking

Thinking error	Examples
❖ Black and white thinking (also referred to as 'all or nothing' thinking	I am either totally safe in the car OR I am in grave danger
❖ Jumping to conclusions	That car would have hit us if I hadn't of told you to slow down
❖ Catastrophising	Any trip on the motorway will lead to a crash
❖ Magnification and minimization	The road is FULL of bad drivers
❖ Personalisation	I'm an unlucky person, if anyone will be in another crash its bound to be me
❖ Emotional reasoning	I FEEL like we're going to be in an accident therefore we should avoid driving today

Worksheet 4 – Cost-benefit analysis of perfectionism

Advantages of perfectionist standards towards other road users	Disadvantages of perfectionist standards towards other road users

Table 3 - The stages of anxiety maintenance

Before the event	During the event	After the event
What I tell myself will happen What I imagine I or the situation will look like The things I do which I believe help me cope	What I say to myself about what is happening Where I place my focus of attention The things I do which I believe keep me safe	What I tell myself about the outcome What parts of the event I recall and focus on How I think this applies to the same situation in the future

Example mindfulness script for driving or travelling as a car passenger

I want you to imagine that your attention is like a camera and at present it is on a panoramic view, taking in everything around you. Just take a moment to be aware of all the things in the environment that is going on. Notice the sound of traffic, notice your temperature, notice what your feet feel like against the floor and how it feels to be sat on the seat. Notice anything that you can smell.

Now I want you to zoom that camera in so that the focus of your attention is on your breath. You are not trying to control your breath in any way, just bring your awareness to the experience. Notice where the breath begins and ends. It may help to close your eyes at this point. Does it start in your nostrils or your mouth? Follow its journey. Does it go down into your chest or your stomach?
At this point you may notice that something else is trying to pull your attention away from the breath. It could be your thoughts, it could be sounds that you can hear, it could be a physical sensation in your body.
I want you to just notice this and guide your attention back on to your breathing. If you have to do this many times during the exercise, that is ok. <u>The skill is in noticing when the mind has wandered not in preventing it from wandering.</u>

Your breath is your anchor to the present moment. Too often our mind is in the past or the future. All we can influence is now. If your mind starts taking you to imaginary scenarios of a car crash then you can use the breath as a way of anchoring your attention in the here and now.

Next, I want you to notice what thoughts are passing through your mind. I don't want you to challenge these thoughts or to make them go away.

I want you to be curious about what your mind is telling you right now. Perhaps it is making judgments about this exercise? "This is boring" "This is stupid" "This is unpleasant" are typical thoughts our mind produces. By noticing these thoughts as just products of our mind we are de-fused from them. If we get caught up in listening to them and obeying them or trying to argue against them, we become fused with their content.

The anxiety that you feel about getting in a car is like a tin can monster. It looks big and scary at first glance yet when we look at it more closely, we can see that it is made up of bits of string and tin cans. Some of the cans are the thoughts that you have when you think about being in a car or that you have whilst travelling. As you sit in the car now, I want you to notice the thoughts you are having about being there.

I want you to simply allow those thoughts to be there and acknowledge that this is just your primitive brain sending out a warning because it is trying to protect you. By recognizing this, we can acknowledge but then let these thoughts go.

I want you expand your awareness to the other 'tin cans', that is, any emotions that you are experiencing right now. If it is boredom, what does this feel like in your body? If it is anxiety, whereabouts do you experience that? Is it in your stomach, your chest, your shoulders? Zoom your camera in further. It can be useful to give this sensation a shape and a colour.

You can breathe into this area, imagine that you are channeling a soothing breath into that area of discomfort or tension. You are not removing the feeling by doing this but containing it.

Open your eyes and expand your awareness back to your environment. Take in the sights, the sounds, the smell. Try to let that spirit of observation stay with you. Be curious about what thoughts will arise during your car journey. If a strong physical feeling shows up, zoom your attention in on. Breath into it.

Worksheet 5 - Creating a Persona

Who does this persona remind me of? (a parent / family member / your anxious child 'self')

_____

_____

What does this persona look like? (is it human form / animal / supernatural)

_____

_____

What does it sound like?

_____

What might I say to this persona to help reason with it / calm it down / nurture it?

_____

Worksheet 6 - Values Assessment

Life domain	What is important to me	Thoughts I fuse with/avoid & feelings that I avoid and which prevent me from valued living

Worksheet 7 - The stages of anxiety reversal

Before the event	During the event	After the event
Alternative thoughts and behaviours	Alternative thoughts and behaviours	Alternative thoughts and behaviours

References

Beck, A. T, Rush, A.J, Shaw, B.F & Emery, G (1979) *Cognitive Therapy of Depression*, Guilford Press

Brewin, C (2006) *Understanding cognitive behaviour therapy; A retrieval competition account*, Behaviour Research and Therapy

Butler, G, Fennell, M & Hackman, A (2008) *Cognitive Behavioural Therapy for Anxiety Disorders*, Guilford Press

Craske, M.G, Treanor, M, Conway, C, Zbozinek, T & Vervliet, B (2014) *Maximizing Exposure Therapy: An Inhibitory Learning Approach*, Behaviour Research Therapy

Davey, G.C. (2006) *Worry and its psychological disorders*, JW.

Ellis, A (2002) *Rational Emotive Behaviour Therapy* in Hersen M & Sledge, W.H (2002) *Encyclopedia of Psychotherapy*, Academic Press

Harris, R (2009) *ACT Made Simple; An Easy-to-Read Primer on Acceptance and Commitment Therapy*, New Harbinger

Lee, D (2012) *The Compassionate Mind Approach to Recovering from Trauma*, Robinson

National Institute for Health and clinical Excellence (NICE guidelines) *Common mental health problems*

Peters, S (2012) *The Chimp Paradox; The Mind Management Programme to Help You Achieve Success, Confidence and Happiness*, Vermilion

Scott, M (2007) *Moving on from Trauma; A Guide for Survivors, Family and Friends*, Routledge

Solomon, C (2003) *Transactional Analysis Theory: the Basics*, Transactional Analysis Journal, Vol. 33, No. 1, January, 2003

Young, J, Klosko & J.S Weishaar, M.E (2006) *Schema Therapy; A Practitioners Guide*, Guilford Press

Made in the USA
San Bernardino, CA
10 November 2018